THE ISSUE OF GUN CONTROL

edited by THOMAS DRAPER

THE REFERENCE SHELF

Volume 53, Number 1

THE H. W. WILSON COMPANY

New York   1981

THE REFERENCE SHELF

The books in this series contain reprints of articles, excerpts from books, and addresses on current issues and social trends in the United States and other countries. There are six separately bound numbers in each volume, all of which are generally published in the same calendar year. One number is a collection of recent speeches; each of the others is devoted to a single subject and gives background information and discussion from various points of view, concluding with a comprehensive bibliography. Books in the series may be purchased individually or on subscription.

Library of Congress Cataloging in Publication Data

Main entry under title:

The Issue of gun control.
   The Reference shelf ; v. 53, no. 1)
   Bibliography: p.
   1. Firearms—Law and legislation—United States—
Address, essays, lectures. 2. Firearms—Public opinion
—Addresses, essays, lectures. 3. Public opinion—United
States—Addresses, essays, lectures. I. Draper, Thomas.
II. Title: Gun control. III. Series: Reference shelf;
v. 53, no. 1.
KF3941.A75I84   344.73′0533   81-779
ISBN 0-8242-0654-1   AACR2

PRINTED IN THE UNITED STATES OF AMERICA

CONTENTS

III. LEGISLATION

IV. ENFORCEMENT

A handgun, briefly defined, is a firearm designed to be operated by one hand; a pistol. This is an accurate description as far as it goes, but it is only when we learn that a crime involving a handgun is committed every two minutes—with a death occurring more than once every hour—that we can begin to understand the deep and passionate responses of those who argue on either side of the debate over gun control.

The December 1980 slaying of rock star John Lennon occurred in New York, a state that passed a stiff gun control law. Ironically, his assailant used a pistol acquired, "presumably legally," in the state of Hawaii. These two facts strongly suggest that if gun control is a solution to the dreadful loss of life our society sustains each year, then legislation on a national level is required. If, on the other hand, gun control is not the answer, and Ronald Reagan among others thinks it is not, then by what other means can society protect its members?

The pro-control argument is that some kind of regulation of the private possession of handguns—the weapon most adaptable to close-range bodily assault—will result in fewer crimes and less human destruction. Of those opposed to regulation, some fear that it would lead inevitably first to a ban on hunting rifles and shotguns and then to other encroachments on individual freedom. Others argue that while the handgun is the cheapest and most versatile firearm for use in crime, it is also the most practical means of personal protection *against* crime.

In this survey of current opinion on the issue of gun control, no disagreement was found on the need to stem the increasing volume of handgun-related violence and also to keep down the rising number of Saturday night specials in society. (Most estimates of the number of firearms in private hands in this country range from 140 million to 200 million.) Where disagreement begins is over the evaluation of evidence—

5

found in books, articles, Congressional hearings, and studies—to support the contention that fewer handguns would indeed mean fewer crimes.

The articles in Section I of this compilation present a broad overview of the gun control controversy and its history. Methods of control are analyzed and evaluated, arguments for and against control are discussed, and the most prominent groups on both sides of the controversy are identified. Gun registration is explored as is the part that gun manufacturers play in the legislation controversy.

Section II is concerned with individual attitudes on gun control. While some public opinion polls indicate that the American public favors stricter curbs on handguns, other surveys disagree. A sample of individual positions is contained in articles by a prominent gun-control advocate, a liberal opponent of control, a hunter, and the Chairman of the National Coalition to Bar Handguns.

The articles in Section III, which deals with legislation, suggest that politicians reflect the mixed feelings of their constituency, but are influenced by powerful pressure groups as well. The section also examines the Federal Gun Control Act of 1968, the 1969 McClure-Volkmer Bill, the Sullivan Law, and the New York Gun Law of 1980.

Section IV deals with the thorny problem of how authorities can enforce gun-control laws once they are passed in the legislatures. While the Massachusetts law seems to be successful in enforcement, the Federal Gun Law of 1968 appears less so. Many of the reasons for the ineffectiveness of existing gun laws are discussed in this final section.

January 1981   THOMAS DRAPER

I. GUNS IN OUR SOCIETY

EDITOR'S INTRODUCTION

The introductory articles in this compilation deal with the prevalence of guns in our society, their easy availability, and the combatants in the battle over their regulation. In the first article, "The Great American Gun War," B. Bruce-Briggs, an historian and policy analyst writing in *Public Interest,* clarifies all aspects of the often emotional debate over control. He cites gun and crime statistics in the United States, comparing them with other nations, and examines the pros and cons of what is called interdiction, "the reduction of the criminal use of firearms by controlling the access of all citizens to firearms." The second article, "Noncombatant's Guide to the Gun Control Fight," from *Changing Times,* is a guide to the contending ranks in the controversy, including pro-control and anti-control groups and government agencies. In this article, the Kiplinger Washington editors estimate that there are as many as 200,000,000 firearms in our society, a projection made credible by rising crime statistics.

The third article, from the New York *Times,* traces a single handgun (No. 519920) in its unencumbered journey from manufacturer in one part of the country to the scene of crime and destruction in another part. In the fourth article, reprinted from *Business and Society Review,* Michael Beard, executive director of the National Coalition to Bar Handguns, discusses the gun manufacturers, their part in gun proliferation, and their resistance to stricter government regulation. Finally in "Have Guns, Will Travel," Jan Reid writing in *Texas Monthly* vividly describes "some of the most terrifying sights in the world" at a firearms flea market, where swaggering gun collectors abound and where anyone can buy a dangerous weapon.

THE GREAT AMERICAN GUN WAR[1]

For over a decade there has been a powerful and vocal push for stricter government regulation of the private possession and use of firearms in the United States—for "gun control." The reader cannot help being aware of the vigorous, often vociferous debate on this issue. Indeed, judging from the amount of energy devoted to the gun issue—Congress has spent more time on the subject than on all other crime-related measures combined—one might conclude that gun control is the key to the crime problem. Yet it is startling to note that no policy research worthy of the name has been done on the issue of gun control. The few attempts at serious work are of marginal competence at best, and tainted by obvious bias. Indeed, the gun-control debate has been conducted at a level of propaganda more appropriate to social warfare than to democratic discourse.

No one disagrees that there is a real problem: Firearms are too often used for nefarious purposes in America. In 1974, according to the FBI's Uniform Crime Reports, 10,000 people were illegally put to death with guns, and firearms were reportedly used in 200,000 robberies and 120,000 assaults, as well as in a small number of rapes, prison escapes, and other crimes. There is universal agreement that it would be desirable, to say the least, that these numbers be substantially reduced. So everybody favors gun control. But there is wide disagreement about how it can be achieved. Two principal strategies are promoted. To use the military terminology now creeping into criminology, they can be called "interdiction" and "deterrence."

[1] Article by B. Bruce-Briggs, historian and policy analyst. *The Public Interest.* 45:37-62. Fall '76. By permission of the author and publisher.

Advocates of deterrence recommend the establishment of stricter penalties to discourage individuals from using firearms in crimes. But "gun control" is usually identified with interdiction—that is, the reduction of the criminal use of firearms by controlling the access of all citizens to firearms. The interdictionist position is promoted by a growing lobby, supported by an impressive alliance of reputable organizations, and sympathetically publicized by most of the national media. Every commission or major study of crime and violence has advocated much stricter gun-control laws. The only reason that this pressure has failed to produce much tighter controls of firearms is a powerful and well-organized lobby of gun owners, most notably the National Rifle Association (NRA), which has maintained that improved interdiction will have no effect on crime, but will merely strip away the rights and privileges of Americans—and perhaps even irreparably damage the Republic. The organized gun owners advocate reliance on deterrence.

The debate between the "gun controllers" (as the interdictionists are generally identified) and the "gun lobby" (as the organized gun owners have been labeled by a hostile media) has been incredibly virulent. In addition to the usual political charges of self-interest and stupidity, participants in the gun-control struggle have resorted to implications or downright accusations of mental illness, moral turpitude, and sedition. The level of debate has been so debased that even the most elementary methods of cost-benefit analysis have not been employed. One expects advocates to disregard the costs of their programs, but in this case they have even failed to calculate the benefits.

The Prevalence of Firearms

While estimates vary widely, it can be credibly argued that there are at least 140 million firearms in private hands in the United States today. This number has been expanding rapidly in recent years. One obvious reason for the growing

gun sales is that the prices of firearms, like most mass-pro-
duced goods, have not risen as fast as incomes. The classic
deer rifle, the Winchester 94, in production since 1894, cost
250 per cent of an average worker's weekly take-home salary
in 1900, 91 per cent in 1960, and 75 per cent in 1970. The relationship to annual median family income has been even
more favorable—from 2.8 per cent in 1900 to 1.4 per cent in
1960 and 1.0 per cent in 1970. More important, increased
competition during the past decade has lowered the absolute
price of handguns. Since 1968, 40 million firearms have been
produced and sold. And these counts do not include the millions of guns brought back from the wars and/or stolen from
military stocks. These figures are usually cited by advocates of
interdiction as demonstrative of the enormity of the problem
and as implying the dire necessity for swift and positive action. But they also demonstrate the incredible difficulty of
dealing with the problem.

    In the gun-control debate, the most outlandishly paranoid
theories of gun ownership have appeared. Some people seem
to believe that private arsenals exist primarily for political
purposes—to kill blacks, whites, or liberals. But of course, the
majority of firearms in this country are rifles and shotguns
used primarily for hunting. A secondary purpose of these
"long guns" is target and skeet shooting. Millions of gun
owners are also collectors, in the broad sense of gaining satisfaction from the mere possession of firearms, but even the serious collectors who hold them as historical or aesthetic arti-
facts number in the hundreds of thousands.

    The above uses account for the majority of firearms
owned by Americans. Weapons for those purposes are not intended for use against people. But there is another major purpose of firearms—self-defense. In poll data, some 35 per cent
of gun owners, especially handgun owners, indicated that at
least one reason they had for possessing their weapons was
self-defense. A Harris poll found two thirds of these people
willing to grant that they would, under certain circumstances, kill someone with their weapon. This sounds very
ominous, but it is such a widespread phenomenon that inter-

dictionists have felt obliged to conduct studies demonstrating that the chance of being hurt with one's own weapon is greater than the chance of inflicting harm upon an assailant. The studies making this point are so ingeniously specious that they are worth expanding upon.

For example, the calculation is made that within a given jurisdiction more people are killed by family and friends, accidents, and sometimes suicide, than burglars are killed by homeowners. In a Midwestern county it was found that dead gun owners outnumbered dead burglars by six to one. Both sides of that ratio are fallacious. People do not have "house guns" to kill burglars but to prevent burglaries. The measure of the effectiveness of self-defense is not in the number of bodies piled up on doorsteps, but in the property that is protected. We have no idea how many burglars are challenged and frightened off by armed householders. And, of course, there is no way to measure the deterrent effect on burglars who know that homeowners may be armed. Though the statistics by themselves are not particularly meaningful, it is true that the burglary rate is very low in Southern and Southwestern cities with high rates of gun ownership. Burglary in Texas would seem a risky business.

The calculation of family homicides and accidents as costs of gun ownership is equally false. The great majority of these killings are among poor, restless, alcoholic, troubled people, usually with long criminal records. Applying the domestic homicide rate of these people to the presumably upstanding citizens whom they prey upon is seriously misleading.

Other studies claim to indicate that there is little chance of defending oneself with a weapon against street crime or other assaults. But almost without exception, such studies have been held in cities with strict gun-control laws. My favorite study was the one purporting to show that it was very dangerous to attempt to defend yourself with a gun because the likelihood of suffering harm in a mugging was considerably higher if you resisted. But the data indicated only that you got hurt if you yelled, kicked, or screamed, but not if you used a gun.

Gun Owners versus Interdiction

All this, of course, is begging the question. Why do people feel it necessary to obtain firearms to defend themselves? The rising crime rates would suggest it is not lunacy. But the data are improperly understood. Despite the high crime rates, there is a very small chance of being attacked or robbed in one's home, or even during any given excursion into the highest crime area. But the average citizen does not make such calculations and certainly would not have much faith in them if he did. He is scared. The gun, if it does nothing else, gives the citizen reassurance.

This last is a reason for large numbers of guns being owned—not quite defense, but insurance. Many people have weapons tucked away with no explicit idea of how they might be used except "you never know when you might need one." No violent intent is implied, any more than a purchaser of life insurance intends to die that year. It is pure contingency.

Apparently most owners care little about their firearms *per se*, considering them as mere tools, to be properly cared for—and, because they are potentially deadly, to be handled with caution. Yet within the ranks of the gun owners is a hard core of "gun nuts" (they sometimes call themselves "gunnies") for whom firearms are a fanatic hobby. To them, the possession, handling, and use of guns are a central part of life. They not only accumulate guns, but also read books and magazines about firearms and socialize with kindred spirits in gun clubs and gun stores. Many such people combine business with pleasure as gun dealers, gunsmiths, soldiers, policemen, and officials of gun owners' organizations. All this is symptomatic of the earnest devotees of any hobby—there are similar ski nuts, car nuts, boat nuts, radio nuts, dog nuts, even book nuts. In this case, however, the "nuts" have political importance because they are the core of the organized gun owners, easily aroused and mobilized to thwart the enemies of their passion.

Polls are unreliable on this point, because internal inconsistencies in the data and common sense suggest that many respondents won't admit to gun ownership, but it appears that at least one half of all American households are armed. They own guns for recreation or self-protection. The principal form of recreation, hunting, has deep cultural roots. In rural areas and small towns, a boy's introduction to guns and hunting is an important rite of passage. The first gun at puberty is the *bar mitzvah* of the rural WASP. Possession of a gun for self-protection is based upon a perception of a real or potential threat to personal, family, or home security that is beyond the control of the police. Very rarely is there criminal or seditious intent. Yet these people are told by the interdictionists that their possession of weapons is a threat to public safety and order, that they must obtain permits, fill out forms, pay taxes and fees, and keep and bear arms only by leave of the state. Inevitably, some of them have organized themselves against such interdiction. With a million members, the NRA is the largest and most effective consumer lobby in America. It maintains its morale and membership by broadcasting the statements in favor of "domestic disarmament" by extreme and loose-mouthed interdictionists and by publicizing the legislative attempts to restrict gun ownership as merely part of a fabian strategy—to use the interdictionists' code words, a "step in the right direction"—toward liquidating the private ownership and use of firearms in America.

The interdictionist position rests on the self-evident proposition that if there were no guns, there would be no crimes committed with guns. But few are sanguine about achieving that situation. Instead, their argument is that if there were fewer guns and/or if gun ownership were better controlled by the government, there would be fewer crimes with guns.

Can interdiction work? Let us examine what is proposed. Guns and control are subdivided in several ways. Usually there is an attempt to distinguish between mere possession and use. Furthermore, different controls are suggested for different types of weapons—"heavy stuff" (machine guns and cannon); long guns (rifles and shotguns); handguns (revolvers and pistols); and "Saturday night specials" (cheap handguns). The levels of possible control can be roughly ranked by degree of severity: market restrictions, registration, permissive licensing, restrictive licensing, prohibition.

Market restrictions seek to limit the number of manufacturers, importers, or retailers of firearms, in order to keep better track of them. As in all areas of economic regulation, a principal effect is to promote the interests of the favored outlets, at the cost of the consumer. They do not deny anyone access to guns, but push up the cost—both the money cost and the personal inconvenience—thereby presumably discouraging some marginal purchasers, but surely few criminals, lunatics, and terrorists.

"Registration" is widely discussed, but no one is really advocating it. To register is merely to enroll, as a birth is registered. Merely to enroll weapons would be costly, to little or no purpose. What goes by the label of registration is actually "permissive licensing" whereby anyone may obtain a firearm except certain designated classes—minors, convicted criminals, certified lunatics.

"Restrictive licensing," such as New York's Sullivan Law, permits only people with a legitimate purpose to own a firearm. Police, security guards, hunters, target shooters, and collectors are obliged to demonstrate their bona fides to the licensing authorities. Typically, personal or home defense is not ordinarily considered a legitimate purpose for gaining a license.

Prohibition is self-defined. If there were no or few firearms already in circulation, a simple ban would be sufficient. But with tens of millions out there, prohibition would require buying or collecting existing weapons or some more complicated policy intended to make them useless.

The preferred program of most interdictionists today contains four elements, most of which have been attempted one way or another in one jurisdiction or another: (1) continuing and tightening all existing laws, (2) permissive licensing for long guns, (3) restrictive licensing for all handguns, and (4) prohibition of cheap handguns, the so-called "Saturday night specials."

The third element is currently considered most important.

Because the great majority of gun crimes are committed with handguns, control of them would presumably promote domestic tranquility. Concentration on handguns is also politically useful. Relatively few of them are used for recreation, so this would seem to outflank the objection of sportsmen to restrictions.

Existing Gun Control

There are reportedly some 20,000 gun-control ordinances in the various jurisdictions of the United States. Most are prohibitions against discharging a weapon in urban areas or against children carrying weapons, and are trivial, reasonable, and uncontroversial. Most states and large cities have laws against carrying concealed weapons, the rationale being that no person has a legitimate reason to do so. In a few large cities and states, particularly in the Northeast, a license is required to buy or possess a handgun, and in a very few but growing number of Northeastern cities and states a permit or license is required to possess any sort of firearm.

At first sight, licensing seems eminently reasonable. Dangerous criminals should not have weapons, nor should the mentally disturbed. But the administrative "details" of licensing become incredibly difficult. It is fairly easy to check out an applicant for a criminal record, which can be a legitimate reason for denying a license. But many criminals, judging from the comparison between reported crime and conviction rates, are not convicted of crimes, especially violent crimes, so the difficulty exists of whether to deny people the privilege of purchasing weapons if they have merely been arrested, but then set free or acquitted. Civil libertarians should be taken aback by this prospect. The question of mental competence is even nastier to handle. Is someone to be denied a firearm because he sought psychiatric help when his wife died?

From the point of view of the organized gun owners, licensing is intolerable because of the way that it has been enforced in the past. One of the peculiarities of most local licensing is the lack of reciprocity; unlike marriage licensing, what is recognized in one jurisdiction is not in another. In the Eastern states it is nearly impossible to travel with a firearm without committing a felony (not, of course, that this troubles many people). Also many police agencies, particularly in the Northeastern states with restrictive licensing, have engaged in some extremely annoying practices. Not only do they load up questionnaires with many superfluous personal questions, but they also require character witnesses to provide intimate information. When the police wish to restrict privately owned firearms, they resort to all manner of subterfuge. In a test of the local licensing procedure some years ago, the Hudson Institute sent several female staff members to try to make the necessary application. The forms were not available and the people responsible for the forms were absent.

Even when the applications are submitted, the waiting period is often deliberately and inordinately long. I have a friend on Long Island who spent three years getting a pistol permit for target shooting. Influence is useful, but even it is not necessarily sufficient. A staff aide to a leading New York politician who has frequently been threatened applied for a permit to carry a handgun as his boss's bodyguard. Even a letter to the Police Commissioner of New York City on the gentleman's stationery was inadequate; a personal phone call had to be made—and that has not speeded up the process very much. The system is not much better with long guns and sympathetic police. Immediately after New Jersey required the licensing of rifles, I happened to be in a police station in a suburb of Philadelphia when a young man came in to get his license. The process had taken six weeks. He commented bitterly, "It's a good thing that I planned well in advance for my Maine hunting trip." (By the way, if he had lost or damaged his weapon during a hunting trip, the Federal Gun Control Act of 1968 would have made it extremely difficult for him to get a replacement out of state).

This sort of anecdotal evidence can be continued almost indefinitely. It suggests to the organized gun owners that licensing systems are a screen not against criminals but against honest citizens, and that licensing authorities are not to be trusted with any sort of discretionary power. It is certainly an inefficient system that dribbles out gun permits and refuses to recognize self-defense as a legitimate reason for owning a gun, while muggers operate with impunity, illicit pistols are exchanged openly on the streets, and penalties for gun-law violations—even by people with criminal records—are very rarely imposed. The Police Foundation is currently engaged in a study of the details of local handgun-law enforcement. Unfortunately, because its head is known as a vocal interdictionist, the credibility of its results will necessarily be somewhat compromised.

Among the most unproductive local gun-control measures are the moratoria permitting individuals to surrender their firearms without fear of prosecution. The police will then investigate such people to make sure they are not wanted by some other agency, and they are then entered in police files. (Obviously, if you really wish to dispose of an illegal weapon, you merely disassemble it and throw the parts from a bridge.) The number of weapons delivered under such programs is infinitesimal. An extension of such programs is the buying of weapons by police departments. This was attempted in Baltimore and obtained a substantial number of guns. But the total collected is a matter of simple economics: Large numbers of guns worth much less than the price offered will be obtained. Few valuable weapons will be turned in—and it is perhaps needless to note that there has been no perceptible effect on the crime rate.

The latest innovation in local gun control is a sort of interdiction through deterrence. Massachusetts recently passed a law mandating a minimum jail term of one year for possession of an unlicensed weapon. This reflects an interesting set of social values, because there are no such mandated sentences for burglary, armed robbery, rape, or even murder in Massachusetts. Every hunter who passes through the state on the way to Maine is risking a year in prison. What is happening is predictable: The law is not enforced.

The Massachusetts experience is both a caution to the interdictionists and a reassurance to the organized gun owners. If restrictive gun legislation is passed, the police will be hesitant to arrest ordinary citizens, prosecutors will be loathe to prosecute, juries will be unwilling to convict, and judges will devise ingenious loopholes.

Most of the existing interdiction laws have been in effect for many years, yet it is not possible to make any sort of estimate as to whether they do any good in reducing crime. Attempts have been made to correlate gun ownership and/or gun-control laws with gun-related crimes, but they are singularly unconvincing for the very simple reason that the data are so miserable—we have no firm estimate even of the number of guns available nationwide, much less in any given community, and it seems that the gun laws now on the books are rarely enforced. Some ingenious attempts to use regression analyses are easy to demolish.

In any event, no serious student of the subject would disagree that regional, racial, and cultural factors completely swamp the effects of gun-control laws. It is true that places with gun-control laws tend to have lower violent crime rates, but it happens that these are Northern communities with a long tradition of relative nonviolence, and the existence of gun-control laws on the statute books is merely evidence of the same relative peaceableness that is also reflected in the low rates of violent crime. The gun-toting states are also the gun-using states and the violent states, mostly in the South. And where Southerners or ex-Southerners are in the North, there are high violence rates regardless of laws. In recent years a few Northern states have imposed stricter licensing and use laws, with no perceptible effect on the crime rate. As with so many things, the laws on the books don't matter as much as their application. People in these states claim that any effects of their laws are spoiled by the spillover of easily available weapons from outside the state, which certainly sounds eminently reasonable. But if the economists are right, the gun-control laws should at least increase the cost or the inconvenience of getting guns, and therefore discourage their use. Retail handgun price differentials between open sources in the South and the black market in New York prove that the Sullivan law does pass the cost of a less efficient transportation system onto the consumer. But we have no idea of the effect of these increased costs upon the demand for guns. Presumably, those who want to buy guns for illicit purposes are not likely to be much affected by an extra $25 or $100 on the price tag.

The spillover effect has led many public officials in the gun controlling states to advocate essentially the extension of their systems of licensing to the entire nation. It is easy to sneer at this approach as the characteristic reflex of failed government programs—X didn't work, so let's try 10X. But the thesis seems plausible. If one could cut off the supply of guns from, say, South Carolina, they would be more difficult to obtain in, say, New York; that is, they would be more difficult to obtain *casually*. So the principal interest of gun controllers is in national legislation.

Federal Firearms Control

National firearms control legislation is a relative innovation. The first important law passed was the Federal Firearms Act of 1934, which was allegedly a response to the wave of gangsterism that swept the country in the depths of the Depression. Originally the Roosevelt Administration attempted to require national licensing of all weapons, but it was thwarted by a previously quiescent organization, the NRA. The watered-down version that passed Congress effectively prohibited (through punitive taxes) the private possession of submachine guns, silencers, sawed-off rifles and shotguns, and other weapons presumably of use only to gangsters. While there appears to be no information whatever on the effectiveness of this law, it seems to have been reasonably successful. Submachine guns are rarely used in crimes. That success, however, may simply reflect the fact that very few such weapons were in circulation, and their rarity gives them too much value to be risked in crime. (We know, of course, that there certainly are tens of thousands of unregistered automatic weapons in the United States, largely war souvenirs. Vietnam veterans brought back thousands of M-16's and Kalchnikov assault rifles in their duffel bags. But most of these gun owners have no criminal intent or any intention of selling such weapons to criminals.) Sawed-off shotguns and rifles may be made illegal, but they are impossible to prohibit; all that is needed is a hacksaw and a few minutes' time.

The second federal effort was the National Firearms Act of 1938. Again, this took the form of a revenue measure, requiring the licensing of firearms manufacturers and dealers. The law requires the firearms trade to keep records of the purchasers of weapons, and prohibits sales to known criminals. But only a simple declaration on the part of the buyer is required. These records are useful for tracing firearms. If a weapon needs checking, it is merely necessary to go back to the original manufacturer or importer and trace it through the serial number to the dealer. Although these records are not yet centralized, *in effect there has been registration of every new weapon sold in the United States since 1938.* How many crimes have been solved through this means, or how it has otherwise been effective to law enforcement, is by no means clear. It would not be difficult to find out, but no one has really tried to. Presumably, such registration is of some help to the police—though it seems to have had no effect on the crime rate or the conviction rates.

The most important national measure is the Gun Control Act of 1968, the immediate result of the disturbances in the 1960s and the assassinations of Robert Kennedy and Martin Luther King Jr. The Act raised the taxes on firearms dealers, added cannon to the list of weapons subject to punitive taxes, prohibited the importation of surplus military firearms and "Saturday night specials," and prohibited the interstate retailing of all firearms. The last provision is the most important. The purpose was to prevent individuals like Lee Harvey Oswald from ordering weapons by mail under phony names. But it also has more annoying side effects. For example, if you live in Kansas City, Kansas, and wish to give your brother, who lives in Kansas City, Missouri, a .22 caliber rifle for his birthday, it is illegal for you to do so. If you are traveling in another state and see a weapon you wish to buy, you must go through the rigamarole of having it sent to a dealer in your own state. So far as one can determine, the law has had no perceptible effect in slowing down the interstate sale of arms.

Enforcement of federal firearms laws was given to what is now the Bureau of Alcohol, Tobacco, and Firearms (BATF) of the Department of the Treasury. These are the famous "revenuers" whose most important function was stamping out moonshining. But for economic and social reasons, the illicit liquor trade is fading and the BATF needs other things to do than break up stills. Since 1968 they have rapidly expanded their funding and activity in firearms control and now devote about half their personnel and budget to that function. BATF seems to be a crude and unsophisticated police agency, more like the Bureau of Narcotics and Dangerous Drugs or the Border Patrol than the FBI or the Secret Service. For example, it says it has no idea how many of the 250,000 licensed Title II firearms (i.e., machine guns, cannon, etc.) are held by police or other public agencies and how many by private citizens; nor has it any information on how many unlicensed Title II firearms were used for criminal purposes. Some of its methods of operating have been irritating to legitimate gun owners. The BATF also made the grave error of providing the organized gun owners with their first martyr. In Maryland, in 1971, a local pillar of the community—a boy scout leader, volunteer fireman, and gun collector—was in his bathtub when a group of armed men in beards and rough clothes— BATF agents—broke through the door. Understandably, he reached for a handy antique cap-and-ball pistol and was shot four times and left on the floor while his wife, still in her underwear, was dragged screaming from the apartment. What had happened was that a local boy reported a hand grenade in the apartment. There was, but it was only the shell of a hand grenade. A simple records check would have been adequate to establish the resident's bona fides, and if there was an

interest in following up the matter, someone might have
come and knocked on his door. He is now crippled for life.
The Gun Control Act of 1968 says that BATF shall have access to the premises of a gun dealer during normal business
hours, which BATF interprets to mean that there must be a
business premises separate from, for example, a private residence, and that there shall be ordinary posted business hours.
BATF also took upon itself the enforcement of local zoning
laws. This problem arises because many gun owners have
taken advantage of simple and cheap licensing procedures to
obtain dealer licenses so they can buy firearms wholesale. The
majority of the nearly 150,000 dealers operate from their
homes.

The organized gun owners see the activities of the BATF
as a plot against them, not realizing that its habits and state of
mind are not much different from other regulatory agencies.
Once an activity is licensed, it becomes a privilege; a citizen
is obliged meekly to petition the regulator for the boon and to
modify his behavior to suit the needs of the bureaucracy. At
the present time, the Department of the Treasury is asking
for a large increase in the licensing fee of gun dealers in order
to reduce the number of license holders—not for any public
benefit, but because it will make the job of regulation easier
for BATF.

"Saturday Night Specials"

The "Saturday night special" is the latest target of the interdictionist. It is identified as a cheap, unreliable, inaccurate,
and easily concealed handgun, allegedly employed for large
numbers of "street crimes." Because it is impossible to define
a "Saturday night special" precisely, the NRA claims that the
concept is fraudulent—but any definition in practice or law is
necessarily arbitrary. Concentration on the "Saturday night
special" has definite political advantages. Firearms enthusiasts scorn it as sleazy junk quite unsuited for serious work.
Nevertheless, the organized gun owners are making an effec-

tive fight against banning the "Saturday night special." They were unable to block prohibition of its importation in 1968, but have resisted attempts to ban domestic manufacture and the assembly of imported parts.

It has been said against the "Saturday night special" that it is employed to commit a disproportionately large number of street crimes, and that getting rid of it would cut substantially into those crimes. A BATF study claimed that 65 per cent of "crime guns" used for street crimes in 16 major cities were cheap "Saturday night specials." Unfortunately, the text of the report reveals that these weapons were *not* those used in crimes but all those handguns collected by police, and anyone who knows anything about how reliable the police are in handling contraband knows that the chances of a quality firearm like a good Smith and Wesson finding its way into the reporting system are infinitesimal. Because the principal sanction against the illegal carrying of guns is on-the-spot seizure by the police, it stands to reason that individuals would pack the cheapest effective gun.

But even if "Saturday night specials" are used for some half of crimes with handguns, their elimination is hardly likely to reduce handgun crime by that much. People buy them because they are cheap. If people want a weapon, and if their demand for handguns is highly inelastic, this only means that whatever guns fell outside of whatever arbitrary definition of a "Saturday night special" that was adopted would sell more. Perhaps this is recognized by the proponents of banning the "Saturday night special," because they have written bills to give the Secretary of the Treasury sufficient discretion to ban all handguns.

Actually, neither side cares much about the "Saturday night special" one way or another. The interdictionists advocate its regulation as a stepping stone toward tight licensing of handguns or the licensing of all guns, while the organized gun owners fear it as a camel's nose in the tent. It is difficult to escape the conclusion that the "Saturday night special" is emphasized because it is cheap and is being sold to a particular class of people. The name is sufficient evidence—the reference is to "nigger-town Saturday night."

Crackpot Schemes

Some other suggestions for gun control are simply silly. One idea is to have all weapons locked up in armories of various sorts, to be drawn by hunters or target shooters when they are needed. But most hunters and gun owners perform ordinary maintenance on their own weapons, so that a storage facility would have to provide room for that. The most overwhelming drawback against the idea is the enormous cost of providing such facilities—no one has calculated how much, and they would, of course, be targets for anyone who wished to obtain illicit firearms.

Another crackpot scheme is to record the ballistics of all weapons, rather like finger prints. This would not be enormously expensive, costing only a few million a year for new weapons only. But it is physically impossible. The pattern that the rifling of a barrel imprints on a bullet is not consistent and can be simply modified by changing the barrel. Ballistics is excellent at a one-to-one comparison between bullets, but cannot be employed for a general identification search.

Perhaps the most peculiar gun-control proposal to date was made by the Department of Justice in 1975. It recommended that, when the "violent crime rate has reached the critical level," possession of handguns outside the home or place of business be banned altogether. This assumes that those areas where law enforcement is least efficient could enforce a handgun ban, and that where the forces of public order are weakest citizens should be denied the means to defend themselves. In almost all high-crime areas the carrying—or at least the concealed carrying—of handguns is already illegal. (Hard data are necessarily spotty, but it now appears likely that the widespread private ownership of handguns for self-protection among crime-liable populations leads to some transfer to criminals, principally by theft. If this is true, it would not seem unreasonable to dry up the demand for guns by providing security to these people.)

The Limits to Interdiction

So the utility of interdiction has not and perhaps cannot be demonstrated. While the lack of evidence that a policy can be effective should make prudent men wary of promoting it, that does not mean the policy is necessarily without merit. Nevertheless, in the case of gun control it is possible to identify some weaknesses in the principles behind the policy.

To begin with, gun control as a general anti-crime strategy is flawed because most crimes, including many of the crimes most feared, are not committed with guns. Firearms are rarely employed for rape, home burglary, or street muggings. On the other hand, a good portion of the most heinous crime, murder, is not a serious source of social fear. The majority of murders are the result of passionate argument, and although personal tragedies, are not a social concern—ditto for crimes committed by criminals against one another. Furthermore, the worst crimes, involving the most dangerous and vicious criminals, will not be affected by gun control. No serious person believes that an interdiction program will be effective enough to keep guns out of the hands of organized crime, professional criminals, or well connected terrorists and assassins. And almost all the widely publicized mass murderers were eligible for licensed guns.

Gun-control advocates grant this, and emphasize the need to limit spontaneous murders among "family and friends" that are made possible by the availability of firearms. But the commonly used phrase "family and friends" is misleading. The FBI's Uniform Crime Reports classify relationships between murderers and victims as "relative killings," "lovers' quarrels," and "other arguments." The last can be among criminal associates, as can the others. Nor can we necessarily conclude that such murders are spontaneous. The legal distinction between premeditated and non-premeditated murder prompts killers (and their lawyers) to present murders as unplanned.

The very nature of interdiction suggests other weakness. It is a military term used to describe attempts, usually by aerial bombing, to impede, not halt, the flow of enemy supplies to the battlefield. Interdiction has been the principal strategy used in drug control; it works only when pressure is being applied at the street level at the same time that imports and production are being squeezed. If there are 140 million privately owned firearms in the United States and guns can last centuries with minimum maintenance, merely cutting off the supply will have little or no effect for generations, and if the supply is not cut off entirely (which no serious person believes it can be), an interdiction policy is hardly likely to have a major effect even over the very long run. To my knowledge, no interdiction advocate has given a plausible answer to the very simple question of how to get 140 million firearms out of the hands of the American people.

Even more to the point, is it cost-effective to try to deal with 140 million weapons when you are presumably concerned with a maximum at the outside of 350,000 weapons used in violent crimes? The odds of any gun being criminally used are roughly on the order of one in 400. For handguns the rate is considerably higher; for rifles and shotguns considerably lower. I estimate that in 1974, roughly one of every 4,000 handguns was employed in a homicide, compared with one in 30,000 shotguns and one in 40,000 rifles. There are probably more privately owned guns in America than there are privately owned cars, and with the obvious exception of murder, the rate of criminal use of firearms is almost certainly less than the rate of criminal use of automobiles. How are we to control the 400 guns to prevent the one being used for crime? And if we decide the only way is to reduce the 400, to what must we reduce it? It must be assumed that the one gun used for crime will be the 400th.

Moreover, interdiction is a countermeasure against crime. Countermeasures provoke counter-countermeasures: Substitution is the most obvious strategy. If guns cannot be bought legally, they can be obtained illegally—organized crime is ready to cater to any illicit demand. If cheap handguns are unobtainable, expensive handguns will be used. If snub-nosed pistols and revolvers are banned, long-barreled weapons will be cut down. If the 40-million-odd handguns disappear, sawed-off rifles and shotguns are excellent substitutes. If all domestic production is halted, we will fall back on our tradition of smuggling. If all manufactured weapons vanish, anyone with a lathe and a hacksaw can make a serviceable firearm. In the 1950s, city punks produced zip guns from automobile aerials. A shotgun is easily made from a piece of pipe, a block of wood, several rubber bands, and a nail.

A more promising variation is to go after the ammunition rather than the gun. Whereas firearms are easily manufactured and last indefinitely, modern ammunition requires sophisticated manufacturing facilities and has a shorter shelf life. Recently the interdictionists attempted to get the Consumer Product Safety Commission (CPSC) to prohibit the sale of handguns on the basis of their being inherently unsafe. This was certainly the most intelligent gun-control tactic attempted so far; yet it failed because Congress explicitly prohibited CPSC from meddling in firearm matters. But a strategy directed against ammunition is also flawed. Hundreds of thousands of Americans "hand load" ammunition at home from commercially purchased shells, powder, and bullets in order to obtain substantial cost savings and to get precisely the sort of load they desire. Shell cartridges last forever and there are untold billions in circulation. Lead and steel bullets can be made by anyone with a stove or a file. So it would be necessary to close off powder sales as well. Smokeless powder would be extremely difficult to make at home, but the old-style black powder that fired weapons for 500 years can be manufactured by any kid with a chemistry set. Besides, any ammunition cutoff would be preceded by a long debate and bitter fight—during which time everyone would stock up. Also, thefts from the military, National Guard, and police would continue to be a major source of ammunition.

The Costs of Interdiction

Against the unconvincing or unsupported benefits of any interdiction law, one must count the costs; practically no attention has been paid to them. BATF is now expending $50 million per annum on enforcement of federal laws. Local police, court, and corrections expenditures are buried in budgets. The only serious accounting of costs was prepared for the Violence Commission of 1968 and was downplayed in the final report. New York's Sullivan Law licensing cost about $75 per permit in 1968; double that for current levels of expenditure; assume that a maximum of half the households in the country will register their weapons; the cost is therefore in excess of $5 billion—or more than one third of the present cost of the entire criminal justice system, from police to prisons. Simple "registration" on the model of auto registration would cost proportionately less, but the numbers are always in the hundreds of millions of dollars.

The financial costs do not exhaust the potential expense of gun-control laws. It is too much to expect government to count as a cost the time and trouble to a citizen of registering a gun, but we might look at the price of diverting police and other law-enforcement officials from potentially more rewarding activities.

But the worst cost is that of widespread flouting of the law. Existing gun controls are now being disobeyed by millions. More severe restrictions will be widely disregarded by tens of millions, including a huge group of stalwart citizens whose loyalty and lawfulness we now take for granted. Needless to say, the organized gun owners cite the Prohibition experience.

The Limits to Deterrence

Organized gun owners, on the other side of the issue, advocate enforcing the existing gun-control laws. I suggest that they do not take this recommendation seriously; the existing laws are not enforceable. Another suggestion would appear to be more credible at first glance—to employ deterrence by having add-on sentences for the use of guns in crime. But such laws are on the books in several states and are not enforced, for a fairly obvious reason: Americans are not concerned with the use of a gun in a crime, but with the crime itself. The murder or armed robbery is objectionable, not the gun. *Illegal gun ownership is a victimless crime.*

Several practical problems make a deterrence strategy extremely difficult. There is trouble putting anyone away these days, and enforcement of existing gun laws or of new laws would add to the overload of an already jammed criminal-justice system. Perhaps most important of all, when the effective sentence for premeditated murder is 7 or 8 years in a penitentiary, how much leeway is there to add to sentences for lesser crimes? Given the advantages of a firearm to a robber, a few more weeks or months of jail is hardly likely to deter him from using it.

The organized gun owners also claim that the widespread possession of firearms in itself deters crime; criminals are likely to be restrained by an armed citizenry. Perhaps—but consideration of criminal tactics suggests the idea is limited in application. Take burglars—by definition they prefer stealth, choosing unoccupied houses. If the owner is at home it is unlikely that he will awaken. A noise that arouses him will also alert the burglar. Should the householder awake, the burglar will probably hear him—especially if he is fumbling for a gun that is, as it should be, secured. In a confrontation, the burglar is alert, while the householder is sleepy-eyed. It is far more likely that a gun will be stolen than that it could be used against a burglar.

In store robberies, the robber also has the advantage. Guns are clearly not a deterrent, since the armed stores are those most often hit—because, to use Willie Sutton's phrase, "that's where the money is." Arming stores will certainly dissuade non-gun robberies, obliging robbers to escalate to firearms. Street robberies offer a similar tactical imbalance: The mugger has the initiative. It is not unknown for even police to be disarmed by criminals. It is true that areas with high gun ownership tend to have less crime against property, but this is probably largely the result of cultural factors. In any event the low quality of data on crime rates and gun ownership makes rigorous examination impossible.

International Experience

Many peripheral arguments used in the gun control debate have little relevance to the issue, but must be addressed. Both sides will deploy the testimony of police chiefs on the desirability or futility of gun-control laws. Liberal interdictionists often cite the testimony of those gentlemen who have most illiberal views on most other law-enforcement matters. Most, but not all, big-city chiefs favor interdiction, while small-town chiefs generally oppose it, both nicely reflecting the views of their political superiors. But, for what it is worth, one can cite the Sheriff of Los Angeles County staunchly demanding stricter gun control laws and the Chief of Police of Los Angeles City saying that public order has broken down so far that only a fool would not arm himself. The gun owners gained strong reinforcement when the Superintendent of Scotland Yard recently pointed out that the number of guns available in America makes an interdiction strategy impossible.

A surprising amount of attention has been paid in the gun-control debate to international experience. In the world of gun control there seem to be only three foreign countries: Great Britain, Japan, and Switzerland. British gun control is taken by the interdictionists as the model of a desirable system. Guns are tightly regulated in the United Kingdom, violent crime is trivial by United States standards, and even the police are unarmed. But, as James Q. Wilson recently pointed out, the English situation is slowly eroding. The key to the low rates of personal violence in England is not in rigorous gun-control laws (which only date from 1920), but in the generally deferential and docile character of the populace. Perhaps it is significant that interdictionists point to "Great Britain" as their model; gun-control laws are even stricter in the other part of the United Kingdom, Northern Ireland.

Japan is an even more gun-free country. Not only does it restrict the ownership of weapons, but it has prohibited the ownership of handguns altogether, and the rates of violent crime are so low as to be hardly credible to Americans. To which the organized gun owners reply that Japanese-Americans have even lower rates of violence than Japanese in Japan.

The third international comparison is used by the organized gun owners. Switzerland has a militia system: 600,000 assault rifles with two magazines of ammo each are sitting at this moment in Swiss homes. Yet Switzerland's murder rate is 15 percent of ours. To which the interdictionists respond that the Swiss have strict licensing of weapons, though this would seem to have very little to do with the thesis that the mere availability of weapons provokes murder and other crimes with guns.

It is not entirely clear what these very different countries—with very different histories, political systems, and national character—have to do with the United States. Those interdictionists who defend civil liberties would be appalled at the suggestion that even the English system of justice be applied to the United States, much less the Swiss civil law or the authoritarian Japanese judicial system—none of which provides the criminal with the rights and privileges he has in the United States.

But let me muddy these waters by introducing two other countries of great interest. Israel is mostly inhabited by a people who have no tradition whatever of using firearms in self-defense and whose compatriots in America are for the most part unarmed and have little taste for hunting. But the objective political conditions of Israel have required them to arm in self-defense and the country bristles with public and private weapons. In addition to the armed forces, soldiers on pass or in casual transit in border areas carry their small arms with them. There is a civil guard in the tens of thousands. Every settlement has an arsenal, and individual Israelis are armed. The government requires registration of all weapons, but the system is very lenient on handguns (for Jews, of course; considerably tighter for Arabs) and very tough on rifles and shotguns, which might be used for military purposes. Israeli gun-control policy is directed toward internal security, not against crime. But despite these restrictions, the Israelis have accumulated huge numbers of privately owned military weapons, including automatics, in various wars and raids. These are held "just in case" they may be needed. But strangely, hunting is on the increase in Israel, as are target shooting and gun collecting, and there is talk of forming an Israeli national rifle association. Needless to say, the crime rate in Israel is much lower than in the United States.

The special conditions of Israel are too obvious to note, but Canada is closer to home, and it is odd that so little attention has been paid it. Since the early 1920s, Canada has registered all pistols on what is essentially the same basis as New York's Sullivan Law. Rifles and shotguns are sold freely, even through mail order. Canada's crime rate is much lower than the United States'. Here, too, cultural factors seem to predominate. It is not usually observed that without the South and Southerners (black and white) transplanted to the North, the United States would have crime rates comparable to other industrial nations. In fact, there is no appreciable difference in murder rates for "Yankee" whites in states and provinces on either side of the 49th parallel.

The best point of the interdictionists is that America is an exception to the international system of strict restrictive licensing. To which the "gunnies" reply that our ancestors came here to free themselves and us from the tyrannies of the Old World.

The Second Amendment

One reason the organized gun owners have bad public relations is that they take an absolutist position regarding the Constitution, relying on the Second Amendment of the Bill of Rights: "A well regulated Militia, being necessary to the security of a free State, the right of the people to keep and bear Arms, shall not be infringed."

To the NRA and other organizations this is an unqualified right, like the freedom of the press, not to be compromised on any grounds. To the interdictionists, the amendment merely guarantees the right of the states to maintain what is now called the National Guard. Actually, the status and meaning of the Second Amendment can be the subject of debate among reasonable men. It is certainly true that the original intention of the Second Amendment was that there be an armed citizenry. A "militia" as understood in the 18th century was indeed the people armed with their own weapons, and the inclusion of the Second Amendment in the Bill of Rights was meant to protect the independence of the states and the people against the threat of the central government's employing the standard instrument of baroque tyranny, the standing army. However, there was no intention of the Founding Fathers to guarantee the use of firearms for recreation, nor for self-defense against criminals (although of the 38 states that have similar "right to bear arms" provisions in their constitutions, 18 specifically provide for personal defense, and one, New Mexico, for recreation).

The supreme arbiter of the Constitution has never ruled directly on the matter. The four cases that have come before the Supreme Court have been decided on narrow technical issues. Three 19th-century cases seem to support the view that states have the right to regulate firearms, and the one 20th-century case, which rose out of the Federal Firearms Act of 1934, was decided on the very narrow ground of whether a sawed-off shotgun was a weapon suitable for a well regulated militia.

Gun-owning lawyers claim that the doctrine of "incorporation" to the states of Bill-of-Rights restraints protects gun owners from state controls. This is reasonable on the face of it. However, the Supreme Court, as it was intended to do, applies the standards of an enlightened public opinion to the law. If the dominant elements in the country favor gun control, it is to be expected that the courts will rule accordingly.

The organized gun owners also see the armed citizenry as a last line of defense against insurrection. This idea has roots in the disturbances of the 1960s. While many Americans viewed the urban riots as the inevitable outcome of centuries of repression, many more merely saw police standing aside while looters cleaned out stores and homes, then envisioned the same happening to *their* stores and homes, and armed themselves. They did not understand that the looting was permitted only so long as it was contained to black neighborhoods; any attempted "breakout" would have roused the forces of public order from their lethargy. Indeed, the contingency plans have been prepared.

The gun owners claim that any registration lists would be used by a conqueror or tyrant to disarm the potential resistance. A minor debate has grown up over what the Nazis did in occupied Europe, especially in Norway. A source in the Norwegian Defense Ministry says the Nazis did not make use of registration lists but rather offered to shoot anyone who failed to turn in his weapons.

But there are examples of the use of registration lists to disarm the public. All handguns were called in following the assassination of the Governor of Bermuda a few years ago. And the late, unlamented regime of the Greek colonels ordered the registration of all hunting weapons, followed by their confiscation, in order to disarm the royalists. Although the guns were later returned by the colonels, the present republican regime is continuing the control apparatus, presumably "just in case." When the IRA began its offensive in Ulster earlier in the decade, the Irish Republic used registration lists to confiscate all privately owned firearms in the South.

Phallic Narcissism

A common assertion in the dispute is that gun owners are somehow mentally disturbed. The weapon is said to be a phallic symbol substituting for real masculinity, for "machismo." The historian Arthur Schlesinger Jr., has written of "the psychotic suspicion that men doubtful of their own virility cling to the gun as a symbolic phallus and unconsciously fear gun control as the equivalent of castration." When queried about the source of this suspicion, he responded that he thought it was a "cliché." Such statements never cite sources because there are no sources. Every mention of the phallic-narcissist theory assumes it is well known, but there is no study or even credible psychoanalytical theory making the point. The germ of the idea derives from the 10th lecture in Sigmund Freud's *General Introduction to Psychoanalysis,* where he maintains that guns can symbolize the penis in dreams—as can sticks, umbrellas, trees, knives, sabers, water faucets, pencils, nail files, hammers, snakes, reptiles, fishes, hats and cloaks, hands, feet, balloons, aeroplanes, and Zeppelins. In other words, any long object can represent a phallus in a dream. Gun owners laugh at the thesis, or are infuriated. One said to me, "Anybody who associates the discharge of a deadly weapon with ejaculation has a *real* sexual problem."

Studies of hunters reveal that they are not much interested in guns or in killing but in the package of skills and camaraderie involved in the hunt. No one has studied the psychology of gun owners or even hard-core gun nuts, nor are there studies of gun phobia. Fortunately, there is a reasonable amount of sociological data available, in the form of public opinion polls, which are believable because they give support to ordinary observation. Gun ownership is more prevalent among men, rural and small-town residents, Southerners, veterans, and whites. Except for the lowest income groups (who may not be willing to admit ownership), guns are fairly evenly distributed by income. Education, occupation, and politics make little difference. Protestants are more likely to be armed than other religious groups. When asked why they own guns, most people respond that they hunt or target shoot. But most handgun owners have them for self-defense, and long-gun owners admit to defense as a secondary purpose of their firearms.

Two generations of good data show that substantial majorities of the populace support gun registration, and this is cited fervently by individuals who prefer not to cite similar data favoring, e.g., maintaining prohibitions on marijuana, having courts get tougher with criminals, and restoring capital punishment. Of course, questions on "registration" are considerably misleading, because no one is advocating the mere registration of weapons, but rather licensing. Most people live in places where there is no licensing and have no idea of the difficulty and expense this would impose upon public authorities and gun owners if the standards of New York or Connecticut were applied nationwide. Gun owners and people with knowledge of existing gun-control laws are considerably less enthusiastic for registration. Supporters of interdiction are more likely to be young, single, prosperous, well-educated, liberal, New England non-gun owners with little knowledge of existing gun-control laws.

The Real Issues

The main point that emerges from any serious analysis is that the gun-control issue, under conditions that exist in the United States today, has practically nothing to do with crime control. I think that there are other issues at stake.

In 1967, armed robbers with pistols killed two policemen in London. There was a wide outcry to "bring back the noose." The Labour government, opposed to capital punishment, responded by extending strict licensing requirements to small-bore shotguns used in rural areas for shooting birds and rodents. In Canada in 1974, there were two incidents of boys running amok with rifles in schools. There was wide agitation to restore capital punishment. The Liberal government, opposed to capital punishment, proposed a far-reaching program to eliminate registered pistols in private ownership and to register all rifles and shotguns. It is possible that gun control is, at least in part, a strategy to divert the mob away from the issue of capital punishment.

Political factors are clearly important. The assassinations of the 1960s and 1970s rather unnerved the politicians. But the wide social unrest of the 1960s probably had more impact. In 1939, George Orwell noted, "When I was a kid you could walk into a bicycle shop or ironmonger's [hardware store] and buy any firearm you pleased, short of a field gun, and it did not occur to most people that the Russian revolution and the Irish civil war would bring this state of affairs to an end." There is a remarkable coincidence between gun control agitation and periods of social upheaval. English and Canadian gun laws date from the "red scare" following the First World War, and the original United States national controls are the product of the violent days of the New Deal.

But underlying the gun control struggle is a fundamental division in our nation. The intensity of passion on this issue suggests to me that we are experiencing a sort of low-grade war going on between two alternative views of what America is and ought to be. On the one side are those who take bourgeois Europe as a model of a civilized society: a society just, equitable, and democratic; but well ordered, with the lines of responsibility and authority clearly drawn, and with decisions made rationally and correctly by intelligent men for the entire nation. To such people, hunting is atavistic, personal violence is shameful, and uncontrolled gun ownership is a blot upon civilization.

On the other side is a group of people who do not tend to be especially articulate or literate, and whose world view is rarely expressed in print. Their model is that of the independent frontiersman who takes care of himself and his family with no interference from the state. They are "conservative" in the sense that they cling to America's unique pre-modern tradition—a non-feudal society with a sort of medieval liberty writ large for everyman. To these people, "sociological" is an epithet. Life is tough and competitive. Manhood means responsibility and caring for your own.

This hard-core group is probably very small, not more than a few million people, but it is a dangerous group to cross. From the point of view of a right-wing threat to internal security, these are perhaps the people who should be disarmed first, but in practice they will be the last. As they say, to a man, "I'll bury my guns in the wall first." They ask, because they do not understand the other side, "Why do these people

want to disarm us?" They consider themselves no threat to
anyone; they are not criminals, not revolutionaries. But
slowly, as they become politicized, they find an analysis that
fits the phenomenon they experience: Someone fears their
having guns, someone is afraid of their defending their families, property, and liberty. Nasty things may happen if these
people begin to feel that they are cornered.

It would be useful, therefore, if some of the mindless passion, on both sides, could be drained out of the gun-control
issue. Gun control is no solution to the crime problem, to the
assassination problem, to the terrorist problem. Reasonable
licensing laws, reasonably applied, might be marginally useful in preventing some individuals, on some occasions, from
doing violent harm to others and to themselves. But so long as
the issue is kept at white heat, with everyone having some
ground to suspect everyone else's ultimate intentions, the rule
of reasonableness has little chance to assert itself.

NONCOMBATANT'S GUIDE TO THE GUN CONTROL FIGHT[2]

Because the U.S. Treasury has charge of money and taxes,
a Washington visitor barely blinks on hearing that it embraces the Mint, the Bureau of Engraving and Printing and
the Internal Revenue Service.

Like all Washington bureaucracies, though, Treasury has
its share of lesser-known appendages: Customs, the Secret
Service, BATF.

BATF is the Bureau of Alcohol, Tobacco and Firearms,
the last of which plunges BATF deep into the gun control
war. And that's just about the hottest, longest-running, most
emotional fight in town.

Consider events of the last year or so. To better do its du-

    [2] Article from *Changing Times.* 33:33+. Ag '79. Reprinted with permission. Copy-
right 1979 Kiplinger Washington Editors, Inc. August 1979.

ties under the Gun Control Act of 1968, BATF planned a computerized system to record by serial number every new weapon and by quarterly reports every firearms transaction of the nation's over 160,000 firearms licensees. BATF figured that this information would help it keep track of the 10,000,-000 to 12,000,000 pistols, rifles and shotguns sold in this country every year and also speed up the identification of firearms used in crimes.

It announced the plan in March 1978.

By April the gun owners organizations that constitute the gun lobby were in full cry against the scheme, damning it as a disguised form of gun registration, which the gun lobby abhors as a first step to eventual gun confiscation.

By May the press was reporting a punitive move afoot in the House appropriations committee to cut Treasury's budget if BATF didn't back off.

By the end of May Treasury was promising that it wouldn't put the plan into effect unless it received specific approval from Congress first.

By the time Congress finished working on the appropriations bills, the $4,200,000 BATF had asked for to put its plan into operation had been neatly amputated.

The formal cease-fire in this particular gun control skirmish came late in February 1979, when BATF withdrew its plan, if not forever, at least for the foreseeable future.

"Gun owners flooded the department and Congress with letters opposing the proposal by an 18-to-1 margin," the Associated Press related.

To the several groups urging gun control in one form or another, this was just one more setback in a series of defeats. They had considered the BATF idea mild enough, maybe too mild. After all, the computer record would not have included names and addresses of those who bought the serial-numbered guns. Nor would it have done anything whatever about guns already in private hands throughout the country, by some estimates nearly 200,000,000 pieces.

The National Rifle Association, on the other hand, had pronounced the plan to be nothing less than "the foundation of a system of massive electronic dossiers on anyone wishing to purchase a firearm in legal commerce" and hailed its rebuff as "a clear victory for every citizen who believes in individual privacy."

Both sides agreed on one point, though: This battle hasn't ended the gun control war. Both sides believe the war will go on.

That Century-Old Impulse

The gun control debate has been going on at least a hundred years. And from time to time it heats up, mirroring some explosive proliferation of weapons or an outbreak of crime or some especially horrifying episode of violence.

To tell the truth, firearms have been as American as apple pie ever since the first settlers arrived. It's said there were as many guns as colonists in Jamestown. Certainly guns were standard household items, both as implements of the hunt and instruments of self-defense, as long as there was a frontier. It is only in the past century, a period of high immigration, rapid urbanization and resulting chronic social tensions, that unrestricted possession of personal arms, particularly handguns, has come into serious question.

The law New York State enacted against concealed weapons in 1866 included brass knuckles but not pistols. Yet in the same year New York City made it a misdemeanor to fire a gun within the city limits and in 1877 passed an ordinance requiring a permit to carry a concealed pistol. Apparently, almost anyone who asked for a permit got one, and some didn't bother to ask. "Let a mad dog take a turn around Times Square," the *Tribune* remarked in 1892, "and the spectator is astonished to see the number of men who will produce firearms."

The truly landmark regulatory statute was New York State's Sullivan Law, passed in 1911. Then, for the first time in this country, a state sought to control—not ban, but control—the sale, possession and carrying of deadly weapons.

The Sullivan Law is now detested by opponents of gun

regulation, but there was scant show of opposition to it when it was passed. Certain events of the day seemed to dramatize the need for just such restrictions as the law imposed. One event was the attempted assassination of New York's Mayor William Gaynor by a disgruntled former city employee. Another was the street murder of a well-known novelist, David Graham Phillips, by a demented violinist.

These incidents did not create the impulse to regulate guns, of course. They merely heightened an anxious public's latent urge to do something about a pervasive climate of fear and violence.

In much the same way, public anxiety, outrage and distress contributed to enactment of the federal National Firearms Act of 1934, the Federal Firearms Act of 1938 and the Gun Control Act of 1968.

The 1934 law emerged from the gangster and the Prohibition years and brought the federal taxing power to bear to regulate the sale of machine guns, silencers and sawed-off shotguns, weapons that one advocate declared, "no reputable person would want or need, and no criminal should be allowed to have." The Federal Firearms Act of 1938, a further reaction to the violence of the preceding years, required that firearms dealers engaged in interstate commerce be licensed and keep records of their transactions but did not require them to verify their customers' identities.

The 1968 law came in the aftermath of the urban riots of the 60s and the assassinations of Martin Luther King, President John Kennedy and Senator Robert Kennedy. This law aimed at more effective control of the ownership and commercial interstate traffic in guns and ammunition, especially the cheap, flimsy, imported handguns dubbed Saturday night specials. Ironically, the law did nothing specific to eliminate the types of weapons used in the assassinations.

Statistical Warfare

Now another decade has passed. The gun control war has cooled except for occasional barrages of propaganda. Anti-gun forces may warn that enough handguns are circulating to arm every third driver a peace-loving citizen might meet on the road; the pro-gun people might react with a fresh alert to their troops to brace for a new attack. The anti-guns urge attention to the public will, as revealed in a 1978 Harris opinion survey counting 80 percent in favor of federal handgun registration, with a 71 percent majority among gun owners themselves. The pro-guns call attention to how a proposal to ban handguns went down by more than two to one when put to referendum vote in Massachusetts in 1976.

The conflict could heat up at any time, of course. It would, for example, if the administration in Washington chose to drive for regulatory legislation. President Carter came to office committed to regulation, and the matter has been pondered in the White House for more than two years. So far, no sign of action.

Meanwhile, the order of battle remains as before. Those opposed to control are united, determined, single-minded, well-organized and well-heeled. Those advocating control are not united, sometimes distracted by other issues, skimpily financed and in disagreement on objectives.

The opposition to any kind of control is monolithic and embodied in the National Rifle Association. The NRA is more than a century old, organized by National Guard officers who had been disturbed that Civil War recruits couldn't shoot straight. For many years it has conducted civilian marksmanship and firearms safety programs, promoted shooting competitions and generally served the interests of hunters, firearms enthusiasts and collectors, and the firearms industry. Its lobbying arm, the NRA Institute for Legislative Action, set up in 1975, does not shrink from describing itself as "the strongest, most formidable grassroots 'lobby' in the nation . . . the only firearms rights organization with a professional team of full-time lobbyists, researchers, writers and attorneys covering Capitol Hill, the White House and executive agencies."

The NRA position is perfectly clear. NRA is against "discriminatory or punitive" taxes or fees for buying, owning or using a gun. It is against requiring licenses to buy or own a gun because that gives some government functionary the say-so on who may or may not have one. It is against registering guns because that would not keep arms out of the hands of undesirables but would make it possible for guns to be seized "by political authorities or by persons seeking to overthrow the government by force."

On the other hand, NRA does not object to prohibiting gun sales to juveniles, applying stronger penalties for using a gun in commission of a crime, and denying guns to convicted felons, drug addicts, habitual drunkards, fugitives from justice, mental incompetents and juvenile delinquents.

Its basic stand is that all citizens of good repute have a right to own and use guns for sport, self-defense and as a final check against tyranny, a right that it says is specifically guaranteed by the constitutional assurance that "the right of the people to keep and bear Arms, shall not be infringed."

Those words occur in the Second Amendment to the Constitution, which reads: "A well regulated Militia, being necessary to the security of a free State, the right of the people to keep and bear Arms, shall not be infringed."

The interpretation of this amendment has become part of the gun control controversy. The NRA contends that the militia comprises all the people and that an armed populace is the last refuge against tyranny, be it domestic or foreign.

Some legal scholars, however, believe that what the amendment is talking about is the maintenance of an organized militia and that the right the amendment protects is not an unrestricted, individual right to own guns, analogous to the right of free speech, but a collective right to bear arms in a military capacity to protect the state, a role fulfilled in recent times by the National Guard.

As it happens, these conflicting interpretations of the amendment's intent have never been put to definitive test before the Supreme Court.

The Contending Ranks

Scholarly dispute about interpreting the Constitution is not the characteristic style of combat in the gun control war, however. More often the argument is strident and each side is prone to castigate its foe for concealing unworthy motives. Some pro-control groups, for example, have painted the gun lobby as a venal, subservient tool of a profit-hungry arms industry. And the gun lobby is given to dark fulminations about conspiracies to disarm the citizenry by confiscating its weapons. When a gun control advocate asks, "How is it that you register your automobile and license your dog but refuse to do the same with your gun?" the standard pro-gun reply is, "Because nobody is trying to seize my car or my dog, that's why."

It is true enough that the gun lobby has the support of the firearms industry. The NRA magazine, *The American Rifleman*, is heavy with advertising from manufacturers and dealers in guns and ammunition. And, though it is a difficult claim to prove, it may be that some proponents of control secretly desire a disarmed society.

There is no doubt at all, however, that at least one prominent gun control group is working toward a society that is free of handguns. This is the National Coalition to Ban Handguns, the organization whose symbol is the silhouetted black pistol crossed out by a diagonal red bar.

The coalition, formed in 1974, is an umbrella organization of more than 30 national religious, professional, educational and citizen groups. Lobbying in Washington is its method, and its stated goal is "the orderly elimination of all handguns from U.S. society." It wants to end handgun importation, manufacture, sale, transfer, ownership, possession and use by the general public.

"There would be reasonable exception," it notes, for "the military, the police, security officers and pistol clubs—where guns would be kept on the club's premises under secure conditions. Gun dealers would also be permitted to trade in antique weapons kept and sold in unfirable condition."

Another pro-control group, Handgun Control, Inc., is a citizen membership organization, formerly known as the National Council to Control Handguns. It endeavors to speak principally for the victims of handgun violence, past and potential. To this end it makes special efforts to organize students and maintains a continuing "handgun body count," tabulating assault, accident and suicide fatalities.

It does not advocate a ban, even on handguns. Instead it advocates an end to manufacture, sale and importation of Saturday night specials, adoption of systems that would make it possible to trace handgun ownership as quickly and easily as tracing automobile ownership, better identification of would-be handgun purchasers, the requirement of a license to carry a handgun outside one's home or business, and stronger penalties for handgun abuses.

Handgun Control's chairman, Nelson T. Shields III, came by his views in the hardest possible way. His 23-year-old son Nick was killed by a handgun in 1974, the last victim in the random San Francisco "Zebra" killings. Shields was for a handgun ban at first but in time concluded that this position was "not politically realistic, practical or enforceable."

The oldest (and smallest) gun control group on the national scene is the National Council for a Responsible Firearms Policy, founded in 1967 and headed until his death in 1978 by James V. Bennett, a longtime director of the Federal Bureau of Prisons.

It takes a determinedly commonsensical midground stance and views itself as neither pro-gun nor anti-gun. It has never advocated a gun ban, even as a long-range goal, and its executive director, David J. Steinberg, calls a ban on any guns, including handguns, "inequitable, impractical and unattainable."

"What is needed and achievable," Steinberg says, "is a policy requiring a license for legal possession of a gun and holding legal owners strictly accountable for the safe keeping, proper use and proper transfer of every gun they own."

So those are the forces in conflict on this long-disputed

battlefield. And you may be forgiven if the dust of battle makes it hard for you to discern just what the fight is all about.

Is the issue guns? Is it crime? Is it guns and crime on one side, individual liberty on the other? All of the above? Or what?

One thing is certain. Few manage to watch this struggle and remain indifferent. Even the outwardly unconcerned have unspoken convictions. Maybe getting those convictions into the open is the only way to resolve this extended, troubling controversy.

Gun Control Groups—For and Against

Organizations interested in the gun control question are numerous. Many are state or local groups, ranging from local gun clubs to groups organized to lobby for or against control issues in state legislatures.

The organizations listed below are merely some of the most conspicuous of those operating on the national level, primarily in Washington, D.C., although most have branches throughout the country.

Any of them would be pleased to provide you with information on their viewpoints, and any would welcome your support.

—*National Rifle Association,* 1600 Rhode Island Ave., N.W., Washington, D.C. 20036 (202 783-6505); Harlon B. Carter, executive vice-president. The foremost organization representing gun owners and the resistance to gun control.

—*Gun Owners of America,* 101 S. Whiting St., Suite 112, Alexandria, Va. 22304 (703 370-5000). Campaigns against politicians who favor gun control and for those who oppose it.

—*National Council for a Responsible Firearms Policy, Inc.,* 7216 Stafford Rd., Alexandria, Va. 22307 (202 785-3772). For licensing gun owners and registering guns. Does not support gun bans.

—*Handgun Control, Inc.,* 810 Eighteenth St., N.W., Washington, D.C. 20006 (202 638-4723); Nelson T. Shields III, chairman. For better identification of handguns and owners, better screening of would-be owners, licensing carrying handguns, against sale of Saturday night specials.

—*National Coalition to Ban Handguns,* 100 Maryland Ave., N.E., Washington, D.C. 20002 (202 544-7190); Michael K. Beard, executive director. A group of organizations working for outright ban on making, selling, importing and owning handguns.

HISTORY OF A HANDGUN, FROM FACTORY TO FELONY[3]

In April 1967, a blue steel revolver rolled off the assembly line at the 100-acre, barbed-wire-enclosed Smith & Wesson factory in Springfield, Massachusetts. Hundreds of people worked on the gun, with the serial number 519920, from its beginnings as a piece of high-grade industrial steel through its six-month transformation into a finely machined handgun capable of firing five .38-caliber bullets in rapid succession.

The revolver was taken from the high-security assembly area, where technicians had fit together more than 150 individual parts ranging from high-precision springs to individually carved wooden grips. It was fired for accuracy, given a final tuning by target specialists and, finally, No. 519920 was entered into the registers the company has kept since it was established in 1852.

The revolver was then taken to a warehouse, packed and logged out to one of Smith & Wesson's distributors. It was one of several hundred thousand handguns produced by the company that year.

On May 12, 1967, International Distributors, at 7290 Southwest 42d Street in Miami, received a shipment of Smith & Wesson revolvers. In the shipment was No. 519920.

[3] Article from the New York *Times.* II, 6:3. Mr. 31, '80. © 1980 by The New York Times Company. Reprinted by permission.

Five days later, International Distributors filled a handgun order for a Denver retailer. On May 17, 1967, No. 519920 arrived at the Wedgles Music and Loan Company, a combination musical-instrument and pawn shop, then at 1648 Larimar Street in Denver. The gun remained there for nearly eight months.

No. 519920 Purchased in Denver

In the first week of January 1968, Norbert Berger, a construction worker, purchased a .38-caliber revolver, No. 519920, from the Wedgles Music and Loan Company for $70. Colorado law requires the purchaser of a gun to demonstrate proof of state residency, and Mr. Berger presented his driver's license. Mr. Berger carried the gun to work with him on January 20, 1968. At a lunch break that day on a construction site in downtown Denver, Mr. Berger wrapped the gun in his coat, put the bundle on a bench and went to get a sandwich. When he returned, Mr. Berger later told the police, his revolver was gone.

Mr. Berger said he suspected a fellow worker of stealing the gun. The police investigated, but made no arrests.

Ten years later, in New York City in the summer of 1978, a man named James John Johnson Jr. unexpectedly encountered in a Harlem apartment building a man he suspected of raping a woman he knew. A struggle ensued, and Mr. Johnson overpowered the other man and fled with a gun the man had been carrying, according to law enforcement officials. The gun was a .38-caliber Smith & Wesson revolver, No. 519920.

How the gun got from Denver to New York and what happened to it from 1968 to 1978 is not clear. The police believe there was a steady traffic of stolen guns from Denver to New York. For example, a number of guns found after a July 1978 explosion in the Queens apartment of a suspected member of a Puerto Rican terrorist group, the F.A.L.N., were traced to Denver by the police. And the man Mr. Berger, the Denver construction worker, believed stole his gun is thought by the police to be linked to a group sympathetic to the

F.A.L.N., whose initials stand for Fuerzas Armadas de Liberácion Nacional, or Armed Forces of National Liberation. But there the trail seems to vanish.

Living in Halfway House

Mr. Johnson, a 53-year-old convicted bank robber, was living in a Federal halfway house on West 54th Street to prepare him for the transition from prison to civilian life. He had just served seven years of a 20-year sentence for a 1971 bank robbery in South Carolina. From 1959 to 1969, Mr. Johnson served a sentence for a New York City bank robbery.

Late in the evening of August 16, 1978, Mr. Johnson, the police believe, walked into a check-cashing store on Fennimore Street in Brooklyn and announced a holdup. The security guard, 62-year-old Michael Penucci, a retired police officer, attempted to prevent the robbery, but was shot and wounded before he could draw his gun. Mr. Johnson grabbed the guard's gun as he fled from the store, according to the police.

A month later, Lloyd Nelson Jones, 34, who had served time for bank robbery in Federal penitentiaries with Mr. Johnson, flew to New York from New Orleans, reportedly at Mr. Johnson's urging.

Shortly before 2 P.M. on September 18, Mr. Johnson and Mr. Jones double-parked in front of the Metropolitan Museum of Art. They were approached by Police Officer Albert Guarineri, who asked Mr. Johnson, the driver, for the car's registration papers. It was a routine check. When Mr. Johnson was asked to step out of his car by Officer Guarineri, he gave the Smith & Wesson revolver to Mr. Jones, and he put in his belt the gun that had been taken from the guard in the Brooklyn robbery.

Officer Shot in Chest

As the officer began to examine the registration forms, Mr. Johnson shot Officer Guarineri once in the chest. Then Mr.

Jones leaped from the car, firing wildly at the officer. In his hand was Smith & Wesson's No. 519920.

When the officer—wounded but not dead—collapsed to the pavement, the two men jumped back into their car and sped uptown as police cars gave chase. They were next observed by the police at 96th Street and Park Avenue, parked in front of a supermarket. Mr. Johnson and Mr. Jones leaped from the car, fired a fusillade of shots at seven police officers who were emerging from a police van and dashed into a nearby apartment building. There they took the elevator to the ninth floor and forced their way into an apartment.

After an hour of fending off police pleas to surrender, they gave themselves up.

On March 17, 1979, in State Supreme Court in Manhattan, Mr. Johnson received five separate sentences of 25 years to life in prison for the attempted murder of Officer Guarineri and seven other police officers. His companion, Mr. Jones, received four sentences of 15 years to life on the same charges.

No. 519920 is in the safe at the Manhattan District Attorney's office. It will be melted down for scrap later this year.

SHOWDOWN WITH THE GUN GANG[4]

The gun companies in the United States are a major industry, with annual sales of approximately $1 billion. Yet despite the controversial and dangerous types of products which it sells, the gun industry so far has been successful in fending off government regulation. Together with the National Rifle Association, one of the most powerful lobbies in the country, the firearms industry has used money and political muscle to fight

[4] From article entitled "Showdown With the Gun Gang at Gun Control Corral," by Michael K. Beard, executive director of the National Coalition to Bar Handguns. *Business and Society Review*. Fall '77. Page 67+. Reprinted by permission. Copyright © 1977, *Warren, Gorham and Lamont Inc., 210 South Street, Boston, Mass.* All rights reserved.

gun control legislation on every front and at every level of government. As a result, the United States is the only modern democratic society without effective gun control. And it is not entirely a coincidence that our country also has one of the highest murder rates in the world.

Anti-gun groups have been focusing their attention on controlling handguns. For there is now overwhelming evidence indicting the easy availability of handguns as a major cause of death and injury. In addition, public opinion polls show that most Americans favor stronger gun control. Yet the gun lobby thus far has prevented Congress from passing a law to limit or ban the almost unrestricted sale of handguns for private use. Present federal regulation is so minimal that it may as well not exist. And the handful of state laws and local ordinances, which have achieved some reduction of gun crime, are a paltry answer to our national handgun problem.

How do Americans buy and use handguns? At present, the sale of handguns is virtually unrestricted. Handguns are advertised in magazines like *Shooting Times* and *Guns and Ammo.* They are sold over the counter in sporting goods stores. Handgun parts and accessories are even sold by mail order. Yet the handgun is also the most widely used and efficient weapon for committing a crime. Its size and concealability make it particularly useful for murder. . . .

Although the proliferation of guns is bad for America, it is good for the gun business. With an annual volume of approximately $1 billion to protect, the gun companies have successfully deterred federal legislation—the major aim of anti-gun groups. The campaign to maintain unrestricted gun sales has been filled with deceptions and phony slogans and almost everything else except facts. The industry is fond of pointing out that if the law were stringently enforced against offenders in gun crimes, there would be no need to regulate the sale and distribution of handguns. Of course, it is true that if there were little or no crime there would be no need to regulate the sale and distribution of handguns. However, in a nation with a soaring crime rate, exacerbated by the easy availability of handguns, the companies' point seems irrelevant.

The gun industry also argues that handgun regulation would be ineffective in deterring crime. How the companies arrive at this conclusion is a mystery, since regulation of gun sales has never been tried. Sales of many other potentially dangerous products—like drugs and spray cans—are regulated by the government with considerable effectiveness. And even if regulating the sale of handguns did not reduce gun crime at all, it would surely cut the rate at which Americans accidentally shoot themselves and each other.

The companies claim they are not responsible for who buys their products or what they are used for. This serious lack of accountability is reinforced by the industry's privilege to keep its sales records private. The firms supply information to the federal Bureau of Alcohol, Tobacco and Firearms only in response to specific inquiries. The gun companies' yearly production figures are kept secret from the public. In addition, they are not even required to report the wholesale thefts which result in thousands of black market gun sales each year.

The gun companies so far have maintained a solid front against gun control. Last year there was a brief threat to the powerful alliance of gun companies and the National Rifle Association, but the rift was quickly healed. Smith & Wesson, a major manufacturer of handguns, proposed that there be national legislation to license handgun owners. This was the first such proposal ever made by a gun company. The fact that it came from S&W was also startling because, as *Shooting Times* once observed, "One naturally thinks of handguns upon seeing the S&W name."

Smith & Wesson's action drew immediate and vociferous criticism from the rest of the industry and the NRA. Pro-gun activists in a number of states organized a campaign to boycott S&W products. After a national boycott was threatened, Smith & Wesson backed down. The company announced that while it stood by its original proposal, the reaction of its customers had convinced it to "initiate no effort to persuade legislators to adopt our position and (to initiate) no other action to advance our views."

The virulent response of the pro-gun forces to Smith & Wesson's meager compromise was apparently based in the "foot-in-the-door" theory of government interference. It is a theory that dies hard with gun lovers, who see a direct and inevitable route from licensing pistol owners to confiscating hunting rifles and disarming the local militia. Gun advocates are on constant guard against what they consider to be infringements of their Second Amendment "right to bear arms." They hold this position despite the fact that the Supreme Court has ruled four times that the Second Amendment applies only to the maintenance of a state militia and is not relevant to an individual's right to arm himself.

It is now clear that gun manufacturers and most private gun advocates will never support any effective restrictions on the indiscriminate sale of handguns. The Virginia state legislature reviewed a short-lived proposal to ban the sale of small-caliber, concealable pistols and revolvers. H. Earl Price, a retail sales manager for one of Charlottesville's largest gun dealers, denounced the bill in the following terms:

> We have the right to bear arms so that we can overthrow any government that becomes too oppressive. In my opinion, legislation like this is exactly that—oppressive.

If the Virginia bill had become law, would Mr. Price have advocated an armed takeover of the state government?

The overblown rhetoric of the pro-gun forces is effective. The firearms industry and the NRA have spent and will continue to spend large sums of money on inflammatory advertising campaigns against gun control. The alliance helped to defeat a Massachusetts referendum to ban handguns. Smith & Wesson, which is located in Massachusetts, would not disclose its expenditures during the campaign against the ban, but the firm made no secret of its opposition. Analysts estimate that more than $250,000 was spent to defeat the ban; the major organized movement in favor of the proposal, People vs. Handguns, spent about $16,500. A survey subsequently revealed that the most frequently remembered slogan from the controversial campaign was, "If guns are outlawed, only outlaws will have guns."

Such scare tactics, implicitly urging the public to arm itself even more against "outlaws," must not be allowed to succeed. The frightening facts about the use of handguns in America demonstrate clearly the need for gun control. As the Handgun Control Project of the U.S. Conference of Mayors says, "Anyone who chooses to argue that the cure for gun crimes is more guns has simply failed to comprehend the future implications of present trends." Obviously, the firearms industry will continue to support a "cure" which calls for more, rather than fewer, guns. And with their support, American citizens will continue to buy guns and shoot each other at alarming rates. In the words of historian Richard Hofstadter,

> In all societies, the presence of small groups of uncontrolled and unauthorized men in unregulated possession of arms is recognized to be dangerous. A query therefore must ring in our heads: Why is it that in all other modern democratic societies those endangered ask to have such men disarmed, while in the United States alone they insist on arming themselves?

The Pistol-Packers at Remington Arms

The largest manufacturer of sporting firearms in the United States is Remington Arms of Bridgeport, Connecticut, a subsidiary of DuPont. Remington, noted mainly for its shotguns and rifles, in 1976 had record sales of $206.8 million and record income of $16.5 million. Five thousand employees work directly for Remington, in addition to two thousand more who work for the firm under contract to the Army.

Remington's 1976 annual report does not mention the approximately 35,000 Americans who died by the gun last year. Instead President Philip H. Burdett observes, "One of the strangest things about America as we begin our third century is that the free market system is so widely attacked. Business—and hence, businessmen—are pictured as greedy and unscrupulous and preoccupied with making large profits (usually described as exorbitant) at the expense of their customers and their workers. Yet many of those who are most vocal gladly enjoy the benefits of the prosperity the free market system has brought.

"This disparagement of business has made it easy for government to adopt a generally adversary role towards business—to over-regulate, to harass through onerous reporting requirements, and to tax to an extent that threatens the future of the system."

On the life-and-death issues of gun control and hunting restrictions, Burdett comments, "The anti-gun and anti-hunting movements continue to pose threats to our business. However, there are a number of organizations which are doing an excellent job of improving public understanding about hunting and shooting. Our own public relations and advertising programs also devote considerable effort to improving public understanding of wildlife conservation and the shooting sports."

HAVE GUNS, WILL TRAVEL[5]

In the southern, midwestern, and southwestern states with the most lenient firearm statutes, gun shows amount to an ongoing circuit of weekend fairs. Advertised as portable museums, they function as hardware flea markets. The governing premise is to exchange guns and accessories for currency, hand over fist. Billed as "the biggest in the world," the Summer Houston Gun Show last August loaded 1700 tables with an arsenal that would be the envy of some governments. On sale were hunting rifles of every description, Magnum revolvers, automatic and single-shot pistols, sealed cases of ammuni-

[5] Article by Jan Reid, M.A. in American Studies from University of Texas and, for several years, reporter on a small Texas newspaper. *Texas Monthly.* 7:101+. Mr. '79. Reprinted with permission from the March 1979 issue of TEXAS MONTHLY. Copyright 1979 by TEXAS MONTHLY.

tion, and large bins of spare parts. Outnumbering the antique flintlocks were obsolete or surplus weapons of recent American wars—M-1 Garands, .30-caliber carbines, even Browning automatic rifles, M-14s, and the M-16s first used in Viet Nam. . . .

Sales pitches varied. One red-faced, jovial man shouted and shook a cylindrical rattle (patent pending) that he swore sounded just like the clash of deer antlers. Others sat back with their arms crossed and eyed the browsers impassively. A man in a jump suit who was buying a shotgun for his teenage son asked, "Do I have to fill out one of those government forms?" The exhibitor shook his head and gave the man change from his hundred-dollar bill. "There you go, son," the buyer said. "Blast away."

Some of the exhibits were aimed at gun collectors, but others were obviously not. Priced as low as $25, likely to fly apart if too many cartridges discharged in their chambers, some of the handguns on display qualified as the "Saturday night specials"—the euphemism for street murder weapons—so prominent in current gun-control debate. Genuine gun collectors were easy to spot; they fussed over serial numbers, inspected riflings with bore lights, marveled over minor manufacturing variations, and drove hard bargains. "I'd want seventeen hundred for it," said the owner of an early Colt. His customer replied, "I've got one nicer 'n this, and I'm asking fifteen."

The real collectors came to Houston primarily to trade with each other. Most of their transactions took place Friday night, before the gun show opened to the public. Affluent collectors usually have federal licenses ranging from Collector's Class, which merely allows them to transact across state lines, to Class III, which enables them to own and traffic in the machine guns, silencers, and explosive devices ordinary citizens are denied. Any federal gun license means the government is satisfied the dealer has good community standing and a true business interest in firearms. Yet the federal license can become a liability in gun-show commerce, because it requires dealers to transact only on their business premises. In-

side the AstroHall they could only take orders to be filled
later. Their unlicensed colleagues could sell any and every
gun they owned as soon as the customer reached for his bill-
fold. Federal law regulates retail sales of conventional rifles,
shotguns, and handguns, but sales of used firearms by private
citizens are free of legal scrutiny, much like used furniture.

Federal agents and some local detectives hound gun
shows because there are almost certain to be several cars in
the parking lot with trunks full of stolen or otherwise illegal
guns, but the offender most often arrested is the licensed
dealer who couldn't resist the sight of somebody's cash. Collectors complain that being licensed exposes them to entrapment by police and places them at a disadvantage with less
law-abiding competitors. One licensed collector viewed most
of his fellow AstroHall exhibitors with a mixture of amuse-
ment and contempt. "It's a low, broad-based market with a
high, narrow pyramid of quality people," he told me.
"Frankly, I'd like to get some of the yo-yos out of it." But he
defended his own position in that market: "The morality of a
firearm transaction is determined by who makes the sale. Any
money looking for a gun is going to find it."

The collector had the tailored khakis, jogging shoes, and
self-assured manner of the academic he might have become
had he not discontinued his post-graduate studies to make the
most of his family fortune. He asked me not to use his name or
even his hometown; he feared burglars. His gun collection is
stored in an armored vault. "I own virtually nothing but five-
screwed Smith and Wessons that I've never fired," he said,
"and never will, because that would blow the value of them.
My guns are an investment—a sounder investment, I might
add, than stocks and bonds."

He later conceded that his attraction to firearms operated
on a deeper level than that. As a child he ran home panicked
and bleeding after a playmate accidentally fired a bullet into
his liver. I asked if that affected his attitude toward guns. "It
affected my choice of whom I played with," he exclaimed
with a hike of his brows. "I've done a lot of introspection as to
why I'm so fascinated by these things. I've read everybody

from Conrad to Lorenz on the subject. Certainly they are instruments of death, but also of power. I've spent years talking
to people and have come to the conclusion that power is at
the heart of it." He brandished a fist. "The power of the direct
physical threat. Have you ever fired a machine gun? It's a
lusty feeling."

The Houston gun show's average customer was probably a
factory worker out to kill nothing more than time on his day
off, but the bizarre always overshadows the ordinary. One
character dragged a fresh leg wound around in open view. I
trailed another youth who wore cowboy boots, jeans and sus-
penders, and a high-crowned flop hat. He was very fat, and all
his attempts at conversation lapsed into a diffident smile.
Mostly he just pointed to what he wanted and then handed
over the money. Soon the barrel of one revolver was stuck
down the fly of his jeans. Another dangled from the holster in
his armpit; he carried a shotgun on his other shoulder like an
ax. And this was as the show was just getting started.

Some law enforcement officials contend that because few
gun-show salesmen accept checks, record cash receipts, or
require their customers to complete federal retail affidavits,
the guns they sell are impossible to trace. Gun shows become
prime markets for the fellow who needs a gun to stick up the
Seven-Eleven or do a little number on the old lady. Stick
around till Sunday, Houston insiders told me. More than $2
million would have changed hands by then, but the prices
would decline as the closing neared, and so would the standards of the sellers. Then the real spooks would come out.

Yet I had no fear of some maniac jamming a loaded magazine into an exhibitor's M-16 and cutting loose on the crowd.
After a while the sight of so many guns loses its shock value;
they resemble the toys of a child. The gunmen with cold steel
shoved down their groins were just posturing. Here, for an af-
ternoon of fantasy, they could pack their guns and swagger
without fear of a bust or of some other badass calling their
bluff.

But just outside was murder-capital reality. People who
know the streets of Houston are made nervous by the sound of

short-barreled guns. On a concrete ramp I saw two adolescent boys laughing and playing with a derringer cap pistol. In their line of fire, a Houston policeman was completing an offense report in the front seat of his patrol car. He tolerated several explosions, then scowled at the boys. "Hey! You mind pointing that thing some other way?"

II. AMERICAN ATTITUDES

EDITOR'S INTRODUCTION

Polls prove only that Americans are divided on the subject of gun prohibition or even gun control. In this section, attitudes in different areas of the country are examined. A Gallup national poll of public opinion on gun control is the subject of the first article. Gallup concluded that a majority of the pollees favored stricter curbs on handguns. But in the next article entitled "Polls Good and Bad," E. B. Mann, gun editor for *Field & Stream*, stresses the inaccuracy of polls and counters the Gallup findings with those of DMI (a polling organization) and a Chicago newspaper, in which the majority blamed economic conditions and court leniency, not guns, for violence in our communities.

In the third article, our nation's foremost gun-control advocate, Senator Edward M. Kennedy, answers questions posed by the editors of *Field & Stream* concerning his S.1936 handgun bill. The Senator's answers are subjected to the scrutiny of a firearms-law authority, Don B. Kates Jr., poverty lawyer, civil rights worker, and gun control opponent. The fourth article, again from *Field & Stream*, offers a defense of gun ownership from a hunter's point of view. In an article reprinted from *Sports Afield*, hunter Grits Gresham, formerly of the Arizona Game and Fish Commission, reveals what he believes to be the fallacies behind some dearly-held pro-gun control arguments. Finally, the Chairman of the National Coalition to Bar Handguns, Jack Corbett, writing in the *Journal of Current Social Issues*, depicts a society without handguns and insists that "less availability of handguns," means "less violent crime."

STRICTER CURBS ON HANDGUNS[1]

With much of the current debate over gun legislation focusing on the handgun, public opinion in America shapes up as follows:

1. The public is overwhelmingly of the opinion that laws covering the sale of handguns should be made stricter than they are at present. As early as 1938, Americans favored more stringent controls on handguns.
2. Not only do Americans favor stricter gun controls in general, but the specific provisions of a law in the Massachusetts statutes also win public approval. In April 1975, the Bartley-Fox Act was put on the books in Massachusetts. The law provides that a person who carries a gun outside his home must have a license to do so and anyone who is convicted of carrying a gun without a license is given a mandatory sentence of one year in jail.
3. The desire for stricter curbs, however, falls short of support for an outright ban, with 65 percent of the public voting against a law which would forbid the possession of handguns except by the police and other authorized persons.

Among the factors helping shape public opinion on handguns are wide-spread concern over the number of deaths caused by handguns (it is estimated that nearly half of the 20,000 murders in America in 1978 were committed with pistols or revolvers) and a growing fear of crime. The latest Gallup audit on the incidence of crime shows that one U.S. household in five has been hit by crime at least once in the last 12 months, with either property stolen or a member of the household the victim of a physical assault.

[1] Article entitled "Public Favors Stricter Curbs on Handguns But Opposes Ban," from *The Gallup Opinion Index*. p. 20. Summer '79. By permission from The Gallup Poll, The Gallup Opinion Index, Princeton, NJ 08540.

Want Stricter Laws on Sale

Six in 10 survey respondents (59 percent) believe the laws covering the sale of handguns should be made more strict while six percent say less and 29 percent favor keeping the laws as they now are.

Most in favor of stricter laws are Easterners and persons living in the nation's largest cities.

Support Found for Law Similar to Bartley-Fox

Since the Bartley-Fox law went into effect in April 1975, gun-related crimes have declined proportionately more in Massachusetts than in the nation as a whole. According to an article by Donald C. McKay Jr., in the *Christian Science Monitor,* Massachusetts gun-related robberies declined 35.1 percent, while armed robberies declined 11.7 percent nationally.

Retired Judge J. John Fox, who co-authored the law with former Speaker David Bartley of the Massachusetts House of Representatives, contends that the secret of the law's success in preventing gun-related crimes can be laid to three factors: (1) Widespread knowledge of the law; (2) speedy trials required by the law; and (3) the certainty of punishment under the law's mandatory sentence if one is caught carrying a gun illegally.

Two major provisions in the Massachusetts law were studied. This question was asked first:

In Massachusetts a law requires that a person who carries a gun outside his home must have a license to do so. Would you approve or disapprove of having such a law in your state?

Three in four say they approve. Gunowners are somewhat less likely to approve, but even among this group, two in three indicate approval of the provision.

All persons who said they approve of this provision were then asked this question:

Under the Massachusetts law, anyone who is convicted of carrying a gun outside his home without having obtained a license is sentenced to a mandatory year in jail. Would you approve or disapprove of this?

When the results of the two questions are combined, it is found that 50 percent favor the plan—with both the major provisions included.

Outlaw All Handguns?

Three persons in 10 (31 percent) would favor a law forbidding the possession of handguns, while 65 percent are opposed to such a law.

Sharp differences are noted by the background characteristics of survey respondents including region and size of city or community. In the East and in the nation's largest cities, for example, opinion is fairly evenly divided.

While there is a great deal of controversy surrounding the entire subject of gun control and what steps, if any, should be taken to combat gun-related accidents and crimes, there is one aspect of the problem that is beyond dispute—there are plenty of guns in the hands of Americans.

Almost every other home (45 percent) now has at least one gun, with the incidence of ownership reaching 53 percent in the South and 70 percent in the smallest communities and rural areas.

Rifles and shotguns are more popular with the public than are handguns with three households in 10 having either a shotgun or rifle. About two in every 10 have a pistol or revolver.

POLLS, GOOD AND BAD[2]

. . . the accuracy of polls depends strictly on the selection of pollees, and on how the questions are worded. Asking such

[2] From article by E. B. Mann, gun editor. *Field & Stream.* 85:16-17+. Ag. '80. Copyright 1980 by CBS Publications, The Consumer Publishing Division of CBS Inc.

questions as "Would you favor laws requiring the registration of firearms and licensing of firearms owners to prevent criminals from having guns?" of urban groups will bring an overwhelming percentage of affirmative votes if only because most of the people polled know little about guns as tools of sport, think of them only in terms of crime, and are unaware that there are already hundreds of laws (federal, state, and local) prohibiting criminals from having guns. It is from polls like this that the anti-gun propagandists back their claims that "most Americans (some say over 80 percent) want stricter gun controls."

But in 1978, when Decision Making Information (DMI: a West Coast polling organization specializing in data-finding for big business) ran a poll based on open-ended, unslanted questions—"What do you think causes crime in the United States?" and "What do you think would be the best way to deal with violent crime in America?"—less than one percent of the respondents mentioned guns as a cause of crime, or gun controls as a way to reduce it.

To the surprise of many, perhaps challenged by the DMI results, Gallup copied the DMI approach less than a year later with the similarly unslanted question: "The federal government recently reported an increase in the national crime rate. What do you think is responsible for this increase?" Did the results justify Gallup's previous claims that "most Americans want stricter gun control?" No. Instead, this poll duplicated the DMI findings, with less than one percent of the pollees mentioning guns as a cause of crime.

As in the DMI poll, large numbers of those polled (29 percent DMI, 39 percent Gallup) charged the high crime rates to economic causes (high cost of living, inflation, unemployment). Even larger numbers (40 percent DMI, 33 percent Gallup), blamed crime on the leniency of the courts, police inadequacy, or the handicapping of the police by plea bargaining or overstrict procedural regulations.

Still greater numbers (52 percent DMI, 42 percent Gallup) blamed crime on social problems (lack of parental discipline, lack of respect for authority, moral decay, permissive society, or drugs). The percentages add up to over 100 in both polls because most respondents named more than one cause.

It is interesting to note that average Americans, chosen at random and permitted to do their own thinking, attribute crime to the same causes listed as "Crime Factors" year after year in the FBI "Uniform Crime Reports"—in which, despite the widely publicized anti-gun bias of J. Edgar Hoover and his successors—guns have never once been mentioned as a cause of crime. Instead, the FBI listings of "Crime Factors" stress (as did the DMI and Gallup pollees) such factors as density, size, and composition of the community population, economic status and mores of the population, strength and efficiency of the police forces, attitudes and policies of the courts, etc.

Incidentally (and surprisingly), even the U.S. Justice Department has criticized Gallup and other polls showing 68 percent or more Americans favor stricter gun controls. The Justice Department has called those polls "methodologically deficient or substantively incomplete in their examination of weapons ownership, availability, and relationship to violent crime." Unwrap that from its gobbledegook and it is not complimentary! In fact, the Justice Department went further and praised the DMI survey for its "soundness and thoroughness" and for its avoidance of the "methodological pitfalls" apparent in other polls.

You won't see (or hear) these polls in the media, because they don't fit the needs of the anti-gun propagandists. . . .

Finally, one other poll that won't be publicized by the anti-gunners: For its weekly "opinion poll," a Chicago-area newspaper (*The Christian Citizen*) asked the question, "Do you favor gun control legislation?" The "yes" or "no" answers showed 8 percent of the respondents favoring gun controls, with 92 percent opposing them.

Yet Gallup continues its forty-two-year record of anti-gun bias with another more recent poll from which he claims (again) that "an overwhelming majority" of citizens want stricter gun controls. His "overwhelming majority" is 59 percent this time; far below his previous findings: but it is this poll that was so severely criticized by the Justice Department as reported above. Maybe the pollsters had better stick to political prophecies and stop reading answers to slanted questions as "public opinion."

GUN LAWS VS. CRIME[3]

Crime is one of the most complex, difficult, and controversial issues of the moment. In the minds of many, crime means guns. Get rid of guns, the wishful thinking goes, and order and peace will be magically restored to the land. But for all the fury surrounding this issue, it has been little more than an undercurrent during the past months of political campaigning. Almost forgotten is the fact that Senator Edward M. Kennedy of Massachusetts, presidential aspirant and foremost "gun control" advocate among American political figures, has authored a bill, S.1936, that would impose a new and, some believe, dangerous federal regulation of gun ownership. Since this issue is of compelling importance to our readers—and, indeed, to the nation as a whole—*Field & Stream* submitted to the Senator a set of questions designed to explore the most important issues raised by his bill in particular and by the question of gun laws vs. crime in general. This allowed Kennedy to answer at length, in his own words, after mature reflection, rather than hurriedly, or under pressure, as might have been the case in a face-to-face interview with one of our editors.

We then asked an authority in the area of firearms regulation—Don B. Kates Jr.—to comment on Senator Kennedy's answers, much as our interviewer would have probed the answers if the interview had taken place in person. Kates was chosen not only because of his knowledge of the gun issues,

[3] Interview with Senator Edward M. Kennedy (Massachusetts), with comments by firearms-law authority Don B. Kates Jr. *Field & Stream.* 85:10+. Ag. '80. Reprinted from *Field & Stream* by permission. Copyright 1980 by CBS Publications, The Consumer Publishing Division of CBS Inc.

but because as a former civil rights worker, OEO poverty lawyer, and professor of constitutional and criminal law, his general political stance is not far from Senator Kennedy's. Kates recently edited a book of essays titled *Restricting Handguns: The Liberal Skeptics Speak Out,* which includes writings by prominent liberals and scholars who have come to oppose the banning of handguns. The book was favorably reviewed by the New York *Times,* Los Angeles *Times,* and various other periodicals that have generally endorsed handgun prohibition.

The following is an exclusive look at the Kennedy gun law and its potential effect on both gun owners and crime. The questions, answers, and comments are preceded by introductory remarks by Senator Kennedy and Don Kates.

KENNEDY: I come to the gun control question from three different perspectives. First, as one who has witnessed firsthand the tragedy surrounding gun violence; two of my brothers were killed with guns. President Kennedy was killed with a rifle and my brother Bobby was killed with a "Saturday Night Special." I would not be frank unless I stated that my past efforts concerning gun control legislation stem in part from experiencing firsthand the suffering caused by guns placed in the wrong hands. Secondly, as the senior Senator from Massachusetts, I seek to represent the views of my constituents on this matter. As you well know, the gun control issue has been seriously debated in Massachusetts, resulting in the enactment of the Bartley-Fox Law (and, I might add, in the rejection of a total ban on handguns). Third, as Chairman of the Senate Judiciary Committee I recognize the national debate over this issue and the existence of competing interests. As you know, the citizens of New York City view the gun issue in a somewhat different light than the citizens of Wyoming.

During my seventeen years in the United States Senate I have participated in numerous debates concerning the issue of gun control and heard hundreds of witnesses. Prior to the introduction of S.1936 in October of 1979, I offered various bills dealing in one way or another with the issue of gun control. Over the years I have carefully studied this issue and gathered a greater understanding of legislative possibilities and their potential impact. S.1936, the Handgun Crime Control Act, outlines my current position on the question of guns in America. It concerns itself entirely with handguns and not rifles or shotguns. I do not consider this a first step toward some subsequent, more restrictive legislation. And, I believe it can result in a reduction in violent crime, death, and injury without infringing on the rights of law-abiding citizens.

KATES: Contrary to Kennedy's characterization of S.1936, the bill does not just ban new "Saturday Night Specials." Rather, it authorizes a special Commission to ban sale of any handgun, no matter what its dimensions. We have only Senator Kennedy's word (which is not binding on the Commission) that the Commission will ban only "Saturday Night Specials" and never go on to other handguns. In this connection, it is necessary to remember that Senator Kennedy is the chief congressional supporter of the National Coalition to Ban Handguns (NCBH), and that organization vehemently supports Senator Kennedy's new bill. Note that the NCBH's goal is to ban (not just control) handguns. And NCBH's acknowledged policy is to support less drastic regulations in the hopes that they can be extended or expanded to a total ban. In the past, NCBH and Senator Kennedy have proposed laws defining "Saturday Night Specials" so broadly that even a Colt "Peacemaker" with an 8-inch barrel would have been outlawed as a "Saturday Night Special." Even less acceptable is this new proposal, which has no definition at all, so that Senator Kennedy's Commissioners could progressively outlaw handgun after handgun until none were left.

1. FIELD & STREAM: You have frequently called for Congressional enactment of something like New York's Sullivan Law, that is, a system under which only the police, the military, and a few civilians could have handguns. (The civilians would apparently include private security services and a few others to whom the FBI would issue permits, but permits

would be denied to well over 99 percent of present handgun
owners. These would have to turn in their guns, though they
might receive some nominal reimbursement.) But the legislation you have just introduced, though severely restricting the
right to buy handguns in the future, allows present owners to
retain theirs and makes some provision for future purchasing
as well. Does your present proposal represent a retreat from
your previous position or do you still see a Sullivan-type ban
as the ultimate goal? If the former, does this mean a break
with such anti-handgun groups as the National Committee to
Ban Handguns and Citizens for Handgun Control?

KENNEDY: I do not believe you have correctly stated
New York State's Sullivan law. The New York law does not
limit handguns to the police, the military, and security
guards. The New York State law simply requires a license to
possess a handgun. Prior to the issuance of a license, the
would-be purchaser is checked to be sure he (a) is of good
moral character; (b) has not been convicted anywhere of a felony or serious offense; and (c) has not suffered any mental illness or been confined to any hospital or institution, public or
private, for mental illness. In addition, a finding must be
made that no good cause exists for the denial of the license. I
have *not* proposed the adoption of the Sullivan law on a national basis. My current legislation merely requires that a
handgun dealer verify the information currently filled out by
the purchaser on the existing federal form. The check would
be to make sure that the would-be purchaser is not a felon,
drug addict, minor, or has not suffered a history of mental illness. This procedure simply reaffirms the present law—
passed in 1968 with the support of the National Rifle Association.

I do not view the proposed legislation as a retreat from
past proposals. Rather, it is a recognition of the need to develop legislation which can be enacted into law. The latest
Gallup Poll indicates that only one-third of the American
people favor a ban on the sale of handguns. In my own state
of Massachusetts, only one-third of the voters favored a ban

on such weapons. It is not the role of the Congress to enact legislation which does not enjoy the support of the American people. Clearly, such a law would be unenforceable.

My legislative efforts are designed to bridge the gap between competing groups on this controversial issue, to develop a compromise position that is fair to law-abiding handgun owners while, at the same time, reducing handgun crime.

KATES: It is Senator Kennedy who mischaracterizes the Sullivan Law. In fact, it is the same system that exists in England, Canada, and a number of other handgun banning countries. Under this system, civilian handgun ownership is banned *except* to those who have a special permit, which the police are free to grant or deny for any reason or none. Some advocates of handgun prohibition have forthrightly described the advantages of a Sullivan-type system: It diminishes defiance of a handgun ban because permits can be freely granted at first and later progressively reduced or cancelled en masse. This has been precisely the trend in New York City since the Sullivan Law was enacted in 1911. By 1957 the police had decided that neither target shooting nor self-defense (by ordinary citizens) were legitimate reasons for owning a handgun. Thereafter, official policy was that permits were limited to people who "require a pistol permit in connection with the pursuit of their livelihoods," i.e. bank and security guards. This policy had to be held illegal repeatedly by the appellate courts before the Department abandoned it—for a new procedure under which the ordinary applicant waits fifteen months *just to get an application blank* for a .22 target pistol and then a like period for the clearances Senator Kennedy so ingenuously describes.

2. FIELD & STREAM: How many handguns would you estimate that there are in the United States today, exclusive of police and military weapons? What proportion of these weapons would you say are used in murder each year? In other violent crimes?

KENNEDY: The latest handgun data indicates that there

are some 53 million handguns in civilian hands. This estimate may be suspect as there has never been an efficient accounting system of handguns manufactured and destroyed. According to the FBI there were more than 10,000 handgun murders in 1979 and over a quarter of a million other violent crimes involving handguns. I believe it inappropriate, therefore, to use the 53 million figure as a denominator for violent crimes. Recent studies have shown that most handguns used in crime are new handguns—less than five years old. Obviously, only a relatively small percentage of handguns are involved in crime. However, just as we take responsible steps to reduce automobile deaths through licensing systems, periodic review, insurance, driving tests, and certain punishment, so too should modest steps be taken to combat handgun misuse.

KATES: According to available manufacturing and import figures since 1898, America has between 55 and 60 million handguns. Even taking the lower figure, less than one out of every 6,000 handguns is used in homicide and less than one out of every 400 is used in any kind of violent crime. (Note that murderers may, and robbers generally will, use the same weapon in several different offenses.)

Senator Kennedy does not explain how his approach, which focuses only on the tiny fraction of handguns that are misused, will combat handgun misuse. The typical murderer has a long criminal history of irrational violence (generally directed against his relatives and acquaintances). Neither the typical murderer nor the quite different kind of criminal who commits robbery, burglary, etc. is going to comply with an anti-handgun law. So to disarm criminals will require a law that is almost 100 percent effective—a law which goes beyond the 399 unabused guns to also get the 400th. None of our other laws (including those relating to automobiles) are anywhere near 99 to 100 percent effective. It is simply not reasonable to suppose that such a law will be effective enough against the people who misuse guns to justify the enormous costs of trying to administer and enforce it.

3. FIELD & STREAM: According to your research, how many deaths result from handgun accidents in this country annually? How many injuries? If a Sullivan-type ban of handguns could be enforced (leaving only rifles and shotguns for self-defense and sport) what would the effect be on the total number of accidental gun fatalities?

KENNEDY: According to the National Safety Council there were 1,800 accidental firearm deaths in 1978. I am not aware of the number of injuries. My current legislation seeks to encourage responsible handgun ownership. I believe that civil penalties bear further study, since such penalties would help further responsible handgun ownership. I believe every responsible gun owner recognizes the potential danger of the handgun and should take steps to keep it out of the hands of those who would misuse it.

KATES: As so often when "gun control" advocates are questioned about fatal handgun accidents, Senator Kennedy responds by discussing fatal accidents with *all kinds* of firearms. National Safety Council figures indicate that handguns are involved in only 10 percent of fatal firearms accidents (i.e., around 200 every year), even though handguns make up approximately 30 percent of all the firearms in the country and probably 75 percent of all the firearms kept loaded at any one time. What these figures suggest is that the "proliferation of handguns" is actually responsible for the progressive *decrease* we have had in per capita accidental firearms fatalities. In the 1930s violent crime rates were about the same as today, so many law-abiding citizens kept firearms for self-defense. Since handgun possession then was only a quarter what it is now, reliance was primarily on long guns for self-defense; and because rifles and shotguns used this way are both far more deadly and far less safe than handguns, the rate of accidental firearms fatalities was far higher than it is today. Over the past fifty years, as handguns have replaced long guns as the weapon kept loaded in the home for self-defense, the per capita rate of fatal firearms accidents has steadily decreased.

However foolish NCBH or others think it is to keep guns for self-defense, millions of people in our violence-prone society are going to keep them because they are frightened. One major harm from legislation that would discourage people from keeping a handgun for self-defense is that they are likely to turn to long guns—and the fatal firearm accident rate will soar once again.

4. FIELD & STREAM: What figures do you have on the number of suicides annually in this country and how many of these are with handguns? If a Sullivan-type ban on handguns could be enforced, would it reduce the overall rate of suicide? Please explain your answer.

KENNEDY: According to the National Center for Health Statistics there were some 16,000 firearm and explosive suicides in 1977. My own legislation calls for a waiting period between the time when the handgun is purchased and when it is delivered.

KATES: Even the most exhaustive anti-gun study ever done concludes that "gun control" laws cannot reduce suicide. The Eisenhower Commission's Staff Report conceded that any one intent enough upon suicide to use a gun would use some other equally effective means if the gun were not available. This is confirmed by the United Nations Demographic Year Book for 1975, which finds the United States fifteenth in the rate of suicide per 100,000 population. Hungary, the nation with the world's highest suicide rate, has one of the world's lowest rates of handgun possession. It and most of the other thirteen countries that rank above the United States in suicide rates have precisely the kind of Sullivan-type prohibition recommended by the National Coalition to Ban Handguns.

5. FIELD & STREAM: Of the murders committed in the United States annually, how many are committed with handguns? What percentage are domestic homicides as opposed to contract killings, robbery, murders, etc.?

KENNEDY: According to the FBI, in 1978 49 percent or 9,582 of the murders committed involved handguns. The FBI estimates that there were over 10,000 handgun murders in

1979. The FBI for 1978 indicated that some 20 percent of the homicides were felony or suspected felony circumstances while 45 percent were the results of arguments.

KATES: Ignoring the 5,999 out of 6,000 handguns that aren't involved, anti-gunners prefer to harp on the .0009 percent of owners who murder—assuming that more anti-gun laws would reduce murder. But criminological studies that have actually examined this assumption conclude otherwise. From a 1975 federally funded University of Wisconsin study: "The conclusion is, inevitably, that gun control laws have no individual or collective effect in reducing the rates of violent crime." This conclusion is confirmed by independently conducted studies at the University of California (1980), the University of Illinois (1979), and Virginia Polytechnic Institute (1972).

6. FIELD & STREAM: Would a Sullivan-type ban on handguns reduce the number of professional killings, robbery murders, and other "hard crime" killings? Please explain your answer.

KENNEDY: My legislation would have the greatest impact on street crime. First it encourages states to pass license-to-carry laws. If you are caught on the street possessing a handgun without a license, you would face a mandatory jail sentence. If the criminal doesn't obey the law, he faces the consequences. My bill also stops the manufacture and sale of handguns knows as "Saturday Night Specials." Studies show that these are the favorite weapon of the criminal. S.1936 would also require a stiff mandatory sentence for persons using a handgun in the commission of a felony.

KATES: It is unrealistic to assume that robbers, who risk many years imprisonment, would be deterred by the prospect that (if caught) they would get a concurrent year term for carrying a gun. Those who actually will suffer from Senator Kennedy's mandatory sentencing proposal are ordinary decent citizens in high crime areas who carry guns illegally because police protection is inadequate and they don't have the kind of special influence necessary to get a "carry" permit.

Mandatory imprisonment for such people is victimless crime law at its worst. A Chicago judge whose Gun Court handles only such cases has written that the vast majority of defendants he sees have no previous crime record. They are "old people, secretaries, shopkeepers, and others who carry guns because they have been victims of violent crime." Though this judge came to the bench a firm advocate of banning all handguns, he gives such defendants only a modest fine. Senator Kennedy's law would require the judge to send them to jail for a year. Not only is this grotesquely unjust, but the effect on the states' prison systems would be catastrophic. For instance, the New York State system (already faltering under the burden of 20,000 prisoners) would collapse completely if required to house a substantial proportion of all those otherwise respectable citizens who carry handguns in New York City alone.

The National Rifle Association proposes alternative legislation requiring that those who commit serious crimes with guns have a mandatory minimum term of imprisonment. Though this approach at least focuses on real criminals and real crimes, it is not criminologically sound either. Although this approach (like Senator Kennedy's) can deter a certain proportion of criminals from using guns, at least for a while, these laws have nowhere *reduced* the number of actual rapes, robberies, etc. The same number of crimes are committed with knives or other weapons. Thus neither approach has more than a cosmetic effect—except, ironically, that the change from guns to knives may actually be harmful. A robber with a gun is far less likely to have to actually harm his victim; as a result, studies from this country and England uniformly find the rate of serious victim injury to be actually lower in gun robberies than in robberies perpetrated with other weapons.

7. FIELD & STREAM: Many people believe that unless a Sullivan-type handgun ban were somehow enforceable against the entire population, its only result would be that law-abiding individuals would give up their handguns while

the criminals kept theirs. What good would this do? Please explain your answer.

KENNEDY: The legislation is not retroactive. No law-abiding citizen is required to do anything in order to retain possession of his or her handgun. Law-abiding citizens would be allowed to continue to purchase and own handguns under my legislation.

KATES: At least they would unless the Commissioners Senator Kennedy's bill creates decided to use the unlimited discretion given them to outlaw all handguns.

8. FIELD & STREAM: If the kind of people who commit domestic homicides could be deprived of handguns, do you believe such murders would decrease, or would the same or a greater number of such homicides be committed with rifles, shotguns, knives, icepicks, and other lethal household instruments? Please explain your answer.

KENNEDY: As to the substitution of other weapons, a recent study in Massachusetts showed that while there may be a substitution of other weapons to replace a handgun, the danger of lethal injury is not as great. The handgun is a weapon that can be easily concealed and fired. It does not require physical contact with the individual as does a knife, icepick, or club.

KATES: The Massachusetts study says nothing whatever about the fatality of *handgun* wounds. Rather, it compares the deadliness of *all* kinds of firearms to that of non-firearm wounds. Some medical studies have directly focused on handguns, finding them only marginally more lethal than butcher knives and icepicks. Of course firearms as a whole are far more deadly than long-bladed knives. But this is not because of the handgun, which kills only 10 percent or less of those it wounds: rather it is because the kill rate of rifles used in assaults is 35 to 45 percent and that of shotguns is upwards of 80 percent. If only 30 percent of those who now use handguns in aggravated assaults were to switch to long guns instead, the homicide rate would still increase substantially—even assuming that the other 70 percent who would substitute knives and other weapons in assaults managed to kill none of their victims.

9. FIELD & STREAM: Many critics of your legislation believe that an effective Sullivan-type ban on handguns would *increase* homicide by reducing the fear that potential attackers now feel toward assaulting a victim they know or believe to be armed. How do you answer this?

KENNEDY: My legislation will not disarm Americans. The Congress will not seriously consider such legislation. The people do not want it, nor would they support it.

KATES: But this is what NCBH, which Senator Kennedy supports, and which supports his legislation, desires. NCBH claims that handguns serve no useful self-defense or other legitimate purpose. It is interesting to note that prison inmates support handgun prohibition on the opposite grounds: that it would make life safer and easier for the criminal by disarming his victims without affecting his own ability to attack them. Typical of prisoner comment, according to criminologist Ernest van den Haag of New York University, was: "Ban guns; I'd love it. I'm an armed robber."

Some communities have dramatically reduced crime through experiments based on maximizing the deterrent effect of handguns. Faced with a substantial increase in forcible rape, Orlando, Florida, police instituted in 1966 a well-publicized program in which 6,000 civilian women received defense firearm training. In 1967 Orlando was the only city of 100,000 plus population in the United States to report a decrease in violent crime. Rape dropped by 90 percent, while aggravated assault and burglary dropped by 25 and 24 percent respectively. In 1971 publicity for a firearms training program for New Orleans pharmacists was credited by police and federal narcotics agents with causing pharmacy robberies to drop from three per week to three in six months there. In Detroit such a program was carried on by a grocers' association over the opposition of the police chief. The program received extensive publicity, first through the chief's denunciation, and subsequently when seven armed robbers were shot by grocers. Grocery robberies dropped by 90 percent. In Highland Park, Michigan, armed robberies dropped from a total of eighty in a four-month period to zero in the succeeding four months, after police instituted a similar program there.

10. FIELD & STREAM: Many also believe that an effective Sullivan-type ban on handguns would *increase* homicide by reducing the ability of victims to defend themselves against potential attackers. How do you answer this?

KENNEDY: Again, my legislation does not reduce the ability of citizens to defend themselves. They may still buy and own handguns. It merely requires that they be responsible and accountable for their use and care of handguns.

KATES: Again, the lack of specific guarantees in the Kennedy legislation, plus the Senator's strong support for and from the NCBH, makes this statement less comforting than it might otherwise seem.

11. FIELD & STREAM: If you believe that handguns are useless for deterrence of crime or for self-defense, do you advocate disarming the police? What about the Secret Service, which protects Presidents and Presidential candidates; don't all the arguments against the utility of handguns apply particularly to the crowd situations in which these Secret Service agents have to work? Please explain your answer.

KENNEDY: I do not favor disarming the police or Secret Service.

KATES: Curiously, the arguments offered in much antigun literature apply even more strongly against the possession of handguns by police than by civilians. These arguments belittle the value of firearms for self-defense by citing incomplete statistics from two cities where householders allegedly *killed* only a very few intruders. Among other errors, looking only at "kills" artificially minimizes the success rate of self-defense firearms; a citizen has been protected as much when an attacker has been wounded, captured, or driven off without a shot being fired, as when the attacker is killed. But if "kills" represents the proper measure, note must be taken of statistics from Chicago and Cleveland, the only two cities that appear to have long-term comprehensive statistics of justifiable homicide. In both cities, about three times as many violent criminals are justifiably killed by citizens as by police. Thus by the reasoning of the anti-gun tracts, it is three times as useful for civilians to have handguns as for the police to have them.

12. FIELD & STREAM: Because police resources are wholly insufficient to provide individual protection to citizens, it is the universal legal doctrine that the police have no enforceable duty to protect anyone. Thus they may not be sued even if they refuse protection to someone who has been threatened and is later injured or killed. If we were to have laws making it impossible for victims to have a handgun with which to defend themselves, do you feel we should also have laws assuring that police resources will be adequate to defend potential victims and giving them (or their estates) damages if they are not protected? Please explain your answer.

KENNEDY: I am not calling for such a law.

KATES: It is quite impossible for the police—and, indeed, it is not their job—to provide individual protection for threatened individuals. The job of the police is to provide general deterrence by patrolling areas where crime may occur and by apprehending those who have committed criminal acts. Necessarily, the law places the primary responsibility for protecting threatened people on the people themselves. Unfortunately, gun prohibitionists seldom deal with the question of how unarmed people are supposed to defend themselves, nor do those who claim that protection is the job of the police explain how threatened people can get the help they need.

13. FIELD & STREAM: Millions of owners believe that they have both an inalienable constitutional right and an urgent need for handguns to protect their families. Regardless

of whether these beliefs are right, do you seriously expect that these people would give up their handguns if they were made illegal? Please explain your answer.

KENNEDY: No. That is the reason why my bill S.1936 is purely prospective. If a person currently possesses a handgun—including a "Saturday Night Special"—he does not have to take any step to maintain such ownership or possession. The legislation only applies to future transfers and does not deny a responsible law-abiding citizen the right to acquire a handgun.

KATES: Opponents to Senator Kennedy's proposed legislation point out that we already have 20,000 Federal, state, and local "gun control" laws that are effective to the very limited extent that any anti-gun law can control the kinds of people who misuse weapons. The National Coalition to Ban Handguns, which Kennedy supports, has stated that any system which allows the people to own handguns must necessarily fail, and that total prohibition is needed. Since Senator Kennedy himself seems now to recognize that this is unenforceable, it is difficult to see what he thinks his own legislation can accomplish. If, as he says, it will not interfere with the right to own or acquire handguns, it cannot bring about the gunless utopia that NCBH hypothesizes. All it will do is federalize various regulations that now exist in some states and that have universally proven more costly in enforcement resources than valuable in reducing violence.

14. FIELD & STREAM: Insofar as many people presently do not comply with existing handgun bans, please describe specifically how the law you propose could be effectively enforced, since the Constitution forbids government to invade homes, search people or vehicles at random, and adopt the other tactics of a police state? Please explain your answer.

KENNEDY: The legislation has been carefully drafted to protect the constitutional rights of all Americans. It in no way proposes, requires, allows, or generates the need for the type of search and seizure that you describe.

KATES: At least not until the Commissioners used the unlimited discretion Senator Kennedy would give them to ban all handgun sales. Anti-gunners imagine that they can end handgun manufacture by putting the legal manufacturers out of business. But a handgun is as easy to manufacture as moonshine: Pakistani and Vietnam peasants produced perfectly functional copies of regulation military pistols with far fewer tools and energy resources than millions of Americans have in their home workshops. A manufacture ban would result only in a black market supplied by illegal imports and "underground factories." To even partially suppress this will require billions of dollars wasted on a vast army of snoopers and informers, wiretapping, bugging, "no knock" searches, and all the other police state apparatus created to enforce our previous crusades against Demon Rum and the Killer Weed marijuana.

15. FIELD & STREAM: One aspect of your recently introduced legislation is a national handgun registration program. Authorities are generally in agreement that such a program has minimal value for catching criminals and would be inordinately expensive to administer. Would it be fair to conclude then that the only purpose of it is to identify which law-abiding citizens own handguns so that these can be confiscated if and when Congress enacts your proposal for an eventual Sullivan-type ban?

KENNEDY: The legislation does not call for the registration of handguns with *any* government. I recognize the handgun owner's fear of federal registration. For that reason, the legislation requires the handgun manufacturer to keep records of the handguns produced and sold. The goal is to make handgun tracing as quick and easy as tracing an automobile. In this way the police would be able to promptly trace a handgun used in a crime, or to return a stolen handgun to its legitimate owner.

KATES: The idea of gun registration is widely popular because people want to "do something" about crime without realizing that violence can only be seriously reduced by painful, long-term, basic changes that reduce the number of

Americans who grow up willing to use extreme violence. The several states that have handgun registration systems find them to be inordinately expensive to maintain and almost completely useless against crime. Criminals do not register their guns—or if they do, they subsequently remove the serial numbers—nor do they normally leave their guns at the scene of their crimes. In any case, Senator Kennedy's legislation involves not registration, but only additional red tape. Federal law already requires every retail store that sells a handgun to record the name and address of the buyer. These records date back to 1937, and the federal government could collect them if it so desired. But it has never done so because it recognizes that the minimal crime-detection value of a gun registration system is simply not commensurate with the immense cost of computerizing the names of millions of handgun owners.

16. FIELD & STREAM: One thing your presently introduced legislation would ban is the so-called Saturday Night Special type handgun. But these weapons are far less lethal as crime guns, since their short, leaky, low-caliber barrels do not allow the bullet to attain maximum velocity. Since you regard handguns as useless for lawful self-defense and primarily only a tool for criminals, how can you justify a law whose purpose is to prohibit precisely those handguns that are least lethal in criminal hands?

KENNEDY: There has been a great deal of misinformation disseminated concerning the "Saturday Night Special" provision of my legislation. In 1968 the Congress, with the NRA's support, enacted a law to stop the importation of the "Saturday Night Special"; however, the Congress failed to stop the importation of parts and did not ban domestic manufacture of such weapons. My bill merely applies the same criteria on imports to domestic manufacture. A recent study conducted in Florida showed that the "Saturday Night Special" continues to be the favorite weapon of the criminal— approximately 70 percent of criminally used handguns were "Saturday Night Specials."

KATES: I am unable to identify any recent study that contains the finding Senator Kennedy describes. On the contrary, over the past five years crime studies have repudiated the myth of the "Saturday Night Special" as a unique or important factor in criminal violence. The fact is that criminals will use whatever weapons happen to be cheapest and most available—including shotguns, which can be sawed off to easily concealable dimensions. The leading British authority on firearms legislation, Police Superintendent Colin Greenwood, has noted that "the number of firearms required to satisfy the 'crime market' is minute, and these are supplied no matter what controls are instituted." If it were possible to legislate "Saturday Night Specials" out of criminal hands, the only result would be the socially harmful one of causing them to substitute far more deadly high-caliber long-barreled handguns. Similarly, an effective ban of all handguns would only result in crimes being committed with the far more deadly long gun or sawed-off shotgun.

17. FIELD & STREAM: Can you cite other countries where gun legislation such as you propose has reduced violent crime?

KENNEDY: Both Canada and England have effective gun control laws. They are much more strict than the bill I am proposing. In Canada and England there are fewer than 100 handgun deaths each year. Our nation had over 10,000 handgun murders alone last year! My bill is aimed at saving lives.

KATES: Senator Kennedy's reference to England is surprising since anti-gun activists abruptly stopped talking about that country in 1972. It was in that year that the only in-depth study ever done of English handgun prohibition (a study conducted at Cambridge University) was published. It concluded that criminal violence has always been comparatively low in England because of cultural and social factors—not because of anti-gun laws, which it characterized as useless and recommended "abolishing or greatly reducing." It is distressing indeed that a responsible public figure like Senator

Kennedy could be so unaware of elementary sociological learning as to attribute England's comparative freedom from violence to the lower availability of particular weapons, rather than socio-cultural differences. After all, England has not just lower rates of gun homicide and robbery, but lower rates of knife homicide and robbery as well. The rate of murders and robberies in which the weapons used were knives, or just hands and feet, is also far lower in England than here. Does Senator Kennedy think that English criminals have fewer knives—or hands and feet—than American criminals?

As to violence in Canada, Senator Kennedy is quite wrong in thinking that Canadians have fewer firearms per capita than Americans; Canadian government studies show that they have as many or more. Thus the fact that Canada has far less criminal homicide demonstrates that the incidence of such violence is determined by socio-cultural factors, not by the availability of particular weapons.

Also to be considered are countries like Switzerland and Israel where firearm violence rates are considerably lower than in England, although private gun ownership is high in both countries. By the kind of simplistic reasoning Senator Kennedy embraces we could look forward to radically lowering our crime rates by requiring that every American home contain a fully automatic rifle—as most Swiss homes do—or by encouraging all law-abiding people to own guns—as the Israeli government does.

In fact, the determinants of violence are socio-cultural, economic, and institutional factors, which cannot be affected by coercive legislation, but only through long-term, fundamental change. The result of simplistic, mechanistic legislation like that proposed by either Senator Kennedy or the NCBH will be only the wasteful diversion of valuable law enforcement resources. Even more undesirable will be the victimless crime persecution of millions of decent Americans who believe that they have both an inalienable right and an urgent necessity to possess handguns for the protection of their families.

GUNS AND HUNTING: FACT VS. FANTASY[4]

Lay that guilty feeling down!

So you like to hunt, and you enjoy guns. If so, odds are good that you have felt a twinge of embarrassment about one or the other, or both, during the past few years. Faced with incessant antigun and antihunting propaganda, usually articulated by those who have ready access to a mass media predominantly sympathetic to their point of view, it is difficult to maintain perspective.

Get your thinking back on track. The fact that you enjoy the thrill of the hunt, and that you find pleasure in owning and using firearms, should never cause you to feel the slightest sense of shame.

Unethical hunter conduct? The criminal and careless use of firearms? All of us, of course, should deplore these things. But they bear no relationship to legal, ethical recreational hunting, or to the proper use of guns.

The facts are on our side on both of these issues, but we must have these points firmly in mind if the ammunition is to be effective. Tuck these rounds away and use 'em when necessary.

"Guns Are Bad"

Gun Registration—Fallacy: "We register autos; why not guns?" Fact: Automobile registration is automatic. Gun registration is not. It places in the hands of officials the power to deny citizens their constitutional right to own guns, and it is most often used in that fashion. New York City residents, for instance, find it virtually impossible to own a handgun—le-

[4] Article, entitled "Shooting; Guns and Hunting: Fact vs. Fantasy," by Grits Gresham, former official of the Arizona Game and Fish Commission, Refuge Manager for the U.S. Fish and Wildlife Service, past president of the Outdoor Writers Association of America. *Sports Afield.* 181:14+. Ja. '79. Reprinted from Sports Afield Magazine—January 1979 issue. Copyright © 1978 The Hearst Corporation. All rights reserved.

gally. In a city of 8 million people, officials have granted only some 600 pistol permits.

Two other points should be made here: One is that only honest, law-abiding citizens can be required to register their guns. The Supreme Court has ruled, on the grounds of self-incrimination, that criminals and convicted felons who are prohibited by law from owning firearms may *not* be prosecuted for failure to register them.

The other point: Gun registration does not work. There are hundreds of thousands of handguns in New York City—not just the 600 for which their owners have permits. Less than one hundredth of one percent of the guns used in Michigan crime have been registered as required by Michigan law. Of the 84 guns recovered after 185 Washington, D.C. handgun murders in 1973, only 16 had been registered.

Guns Cause Crime—Fact: No study has ever shown that the availability of firearms has any effect on the rate of crime. Switzerland requires that every able-bodied male have a rifle and ammo in his home, perhaps providing the ultimate in firearm availability. Yet Switzerland has virtually no violent crime.

Gun Laws Reduce Crime—Fallacy: "Tokyo's rigid handgun laws and low murder rate prove that such laws are effective." Fact: The murder rate by Japanese-Americans in the United States is less than half that by the Japanese in Tokyo, despite the ready availability of guns to all nationalities in this country. Crime is a socio-economic problem; not one of firearms availability.

The Tokyo and New York City handgun laws are almost identical. The murder rates? In Tokyo—1.9 per 100,000 people. In New York—17.5.

Gun Accidents Cause Many Deaths—Fact: You are more likely to choke to death while eating than to die from accidental gunshot. Shooting and hunting are very safe activities.

"Hunting Is Bad"

"Those bad 'ole hunters have killed everything out."
Don't you believe it.

Hunters have been the leaders in the conservation movement since it began in this country, and they still are. They
were planning and financing research into animal life histories and management techniques, and financing the preservation and restoration of wildlife habitat long before the current crop of protectionists saw the light of day.

Ever hear of a special interest group *asking* for more
taxes? Hunters did it. Over the years they requested and got
the imposition of special excise taxes on sporting arms and
ammunition, on handguns and on archery equipment, with
those millions of dollars being funneled into research, wildlife
management and land acquisition.

One fallacy that often crops up is: Hunters have been responsible for the extinction of many species of wildlife. The
fact is that sport hunting has never been responsible for the
extinction of any species. To the contrary, it's quite possible
that the efforts of hunters have saved several from passing
into oblivion.

Most game populations in the United States are in far
better condition now than they were at the turn of this century, and the programs instigated and financed by hunters get
the credit. A fallout from the habitat acquisition, preservation
and restoration portions of these programs is that nongame
species also benefit tremendously.

Hunters insist on good management of the game species
they're interested in, and willingly pay for it. Which only
emphasizes the point that, if you're a wildlife species, it's nice
to be wanted . . . by hunters.

The ivory-billed woodpecker hasn't been that fortunate.
Never a gamebird, it wasn't hunted, and now it may have
faded from the scene without a shot being fired. Nobody
cared . . . not enough to preserve the habitat necessary for its
survival.

Where antigun and antihunting sentiments are concerned, I seem to see a light at the end of the tunnel. Americans are sorting out the facts from the fallacies. More and more people are becoming convinced that guns do not cause crime and that the hunter is indeed wildlife's best friend.

LIVING WITHOUT HANDGUNS[5]

Not long ago I received a letter from a prison inmate. It said, "Here I am serving thirty years in prison for murder—the best years of my life. Had it not been for handguns, I wouldn't be here. Yes, I'm for gun control." When I received that letter I wondered how many prisoners would be serving long terms in prison if we had a handgun-less society. How many victims would yet be alive?

If ex-policemen were not permitted to keep their service revolvers, would Dan White ever have killed San Francisco Mayor George Moscone and Councilman Harvey Milk? If Sirhan-Sirhan had not so easily secured a pistol from a "friend," would Robert Kennedy be alive today? If certain criminals connected with the drug traffic had not so easily secured deadly weapons, would federal Judge John H. Wood, Jr., have been spared assassination?

Another letter came from a distraught widow. She said that her husband was having periods of depression. One day, in the midst of a down mood, he walked down to the local hardware store, bought a handgun, went home, and shot himself to death. She wondered why such lethal instruments are so readily available to the suicidal. We don't sell addictive drugs to people who shouldn't have them. This is an important concern. There are about the same number of gun suicides each year as there are murders.

[5] Article by Jack Corbett, initiator and chairman of the National Coalition to Bar Handguns. *Journal of Current Social Issues.* 16:20. Summer '77. Copyright 1979 United Church Board for Homeland Ministries. Reprinted with permission.

There is a definite connection between ready availability of firearms and violent crime in the United States. The Eisenhower Commission on the Causes and Prevention of Violence noted this relationship in its 1968 study. In the Northeastern portion of the United States, 33 percent of all households own guns and in the South (including Texas) the figure rises to 59 percent. Interestingly enough, when examining the figures for woundings and murders, the correlation rings true. The Northeast has the lowest rate of firearms crime—14 percent of all assaults and 44 percent of all murders are committed with guns. When one examines the picture in the South, on the other hand, the figures are 25 percent and 72 percent respectively.

There is a problem in the United States with handguns all right. During 1977—the last year for which FBI figures are available—there were 9,178 murders with handguns, 48 percent of all murders. That year there were also 170,037 robberies with firearms, mostly handguns. In addition, 120,177 persons were assaulted with guns in 1977, again mostly with pistols and revolvers. What the latter means is that this many persons were blinded, deafened, paralyzed, dismembered or had holes shot through them in other ways.

To assess the magnitude of the problem, one may well compare the number of Americans killed by guns in the U.S.A. from 1963 to 1973 with the number of U.S. soldiers killed in Vietnam during that wartime period. From 1963 to 1973 there were 46,121 Americans killed in the Vietnam War. Over the same period 84,644 Americans were murdered by firearms within the United States. About 80 percent of these were killed with handguns. Thus, fantastic as it may seem, there were more Americans killed by handguns in the United States during the Vietnam War than there were American fatalities during that tragic conflict. It is a fair question to ask, is there a war going on right here?

Yet opponents of gun control tend to say: "Look at New York City, the crime capital of the world. They have the toughest gun control law in the nation, the Sullivan Law, but it doesn't do any good." Let's get something straight. New York City, on a per population basis, ranks 14th in the nation among major cities in its murder rate (See FBI Uniform Crime Reports 1977). In any case, an article appearing in *New York* magazine by Steven Brill pointed out that in 1973 more than 75 percent of the guns used in crimes in New York City were purchased in Southern states with lenient laws. What has happened in the past is that handguns were purchased in Southern states by the bushel basket and sold for two or three times the price on the streets of New York. Only a stringent national law can prevent that.

The strictest gun laws in the country are in the Northeastern states; the weakest are in the South. The stricter the law, the less availability of firearms. The less availability, the less violent crime. It's as simple as that, but as difficult—because, let's face it, we have had *no* national gun control measures enacted since 1968. And the slaughter continues unabated.

It is a well-known fact that most criminals secure their guns legally by purchasing them over-the-counter just like law-abiding citizens. We make it easy in this country to commit crime with a deadly weapon. To be sure, in some states and municipalities there are waiting periods. But, practically speaking, no police check is made on the purchaser as to his qualifications for owning a gun. The police, under-staffed, are too busy to make such routine checks.

Not only this, but the criminal in America is finding easy access to guns through stolen weapons. We have an odd situation occurring in the United States. A recent Police Foundation study reflects that about 275,000 guns are stolen each year in the U.S.A. They indicate that this is about the number needed by the entire criminal community each year. So what is happening in part is this: The householder buys a handgun to protect his home. The burglar stakes out the house and enters when the resident is at work or away on vacation. The thief steals the silverware and, to add insult to injury, makes off with the householder's "protective" handgun as well. Then he "fences" the gun into the criminal community where it is used against the law-abiding citizen in street crime or in a small shop holdup.

When dealing with this vital issue of handgun control, we need to clarify two troubling questions: (1) Is it wise to keep a handgun in the home? (2) Doesn't the Second Amendment guarantee citizens the "right to bear arms?"

About 50 million handguns are now in the homes of the nation. They are there, presumably, as a protective device. But instead of protecting, these weapons of death expose us to violence. According to the 1977 FBI Uniform Crime Reports, 60 percent of the people murdered were family members, friends, neighbors, or acquaintances of the murderer. Thus, if one keeps a loaded gun in the home, it is much more likely to cause injury or death to family or friends than to an intruder. For every burglar shot and killed with a gun, four to six home-owners or family members are killed accidentally by a gun. So, if you're going to keep a gun around the house, it would best be kept unloaded and locked up.

What about "the right to bear arms?" Is this an unqualified, fundamental, Constitutionally-guaranteed right? No. The Second Amendment states: "A well-regulated militia, being necessary to the security of a free state, the right of the people to keep and bear arms, shall not be infringed." However, the "right" in this particular Amendment refers specifically to the arming of a "well-regulated militia," which today is represented by the National Guard. The U.S. Supreme Court has interpreted the meaning of the Second Amendment in this way. In 1976, the U.S. Sixth Court of Appeals declared, "There can be no serious claim to any express constitutional right by any individual to possess a firearm."

The American Bar Association meeting in 1976 took action to clarify the meaning of the Second Amendment. They said:

In addition to the five decisions in which the Supreme Court has construed the Amendment, every Federal court decision involving the Amendment has given the Amendment a collective, militia interpretation and/or held that firearms control laws enacted under a state's police power are constitutional. Thus arguments premised upon the Federal Second Amendment, or the similar provisions in the thirty-seven state constitutions, have never prevented regulation of firearms.

Nor should they, for as the ABA contends, it is a collective right, not a personal one.

The National Rifle Association has set forth, from time to time, certain arguments which have been effective in opposing the enactment of handgun control. But are they right? Let us examine them, one by one.

When guns are outlawed, only outlaws will have guns. Actually, when handguns are outlawed, there will still be about 150 million rifles and shotguns left among the public in our society. If protection is needed, they ought to be able to provide it. Of course, the police and security guards will still have handguns, and presumably they are not "outlaws." On the other hand, when handguns are outlawed, it will be much more difficult for criminals to get their hands on the weapons of crime. For their normal source of supply—legal sales and stolen guns—will shrink.

Handguns don't kill people, people kill people. Technically speaking, it would be more appropriate to say: "People armed with handguns kill people." If the NRA really believed their popular slogan, they would be willing to place controls on people—licensing restrictions, for example.

Banning handguns would only be a "foot-in-the-door mechanism." The ultimate objective is to make all guns illegal. Proponents of firearms are suspicious that one limited action will lead to another more comprehensive one. It might, but it is unlikely. There is a significant difference between rifles and shotguns, which have legitimate sporting purposes, and the handgun which is primarily good for shooting people. If hunters wish to shoot rabbits, why not use a rifle? Why claim to be dependent upon the weapon of crime? The author knows of no group of any significance which is publicly advocating eliminating long guns. We have to make sophisticated distinctions in our society between sporting weapons and the weapons of crime.

Gun control laws don't work. Actually, to a limited extent they have worked. States with strict gun control laws have had a lower gun murder rate than those with lenient laws. In many cases, state and local gun control regulations are circumvented because persons buy guns in the easy access areas and bring them into the "adequate control" regions. The only way this can be avoided is to enact a decent national law and then enforce it. What has happened in the District of Columbia since the enactment in 1976 of a bill to ban the *sale* of all handguns is that murder has gone down 20 percent and robbery 31 percent.

Banning handguns would in effect mean imposing "confiscation." Confiscation means "seize by authority." That certainly would be unconstitutional, and even the most ardent gun control advocate should oppose it. Practically speaking, probably only those homes would be searched where there was thought to be a store of unsurrendered handguns once a ban was enacted. This would occur only after a respectable waiting period, and a search warrant had been obtained, and the handgun hold-out had been requested several times to turn in his illegal cache.

Most Americans are law-abiding citizens and would turn in their guns if the law so required. Legislative proposals being offered for eliminating handguns from our society generally provide compensation to those who turn in their guns. Thus, the law would tend to be self-enforcing. The key word is "compensation" not "confiscation."

A number of alternatives have been suggested for handgun control. To a certain extent each has some merit. One common suggestion is that mandatory minimum sentences be imposed upon persons who commit a crime with a gun. Proponents say, "Why not throw the book at the troublemakers in our society rather than causing trouble for law-abiding citizens by making them register or secure licenses?" On its face, this approach seems to hold some merit, and it is difficult for those who purport to be for gun control to oppose it. However, heavy sentences seldom deter offenders from crime; they don't think they will get caught. This will deter only the most sophisticated and calculating. When one ponders the fact that about two-thirds of the gun murders in our society are "crimes of passion," performed in the heat of anger, one must discount the value of heavy prison sentences as a deterrent.

Another popular proposal is to ban the sale of "Saturday Night Specials"—cheap, inaccurate, low-caliber type handguns. It is commonly believed that a large proportion of crime is committed with these weapons. There are about 400,000 of these guns sold each year, according to the House Subcommittee on Crime. With some 50 million handguns extant in society, one can see that this step would ban less than one percent. Nevertheless, it would be a start.

Registration is another often-proposed suggestion for handgun control. The police seem to favor it as a means to trace guns. But there are drawbacks. Criminals are not so obliging as to leave their guns behind after committing a crime. Also, a registration system would be administratively cumbersome.

"If automobiles are licensed, why not guns?" say many gun control supporters. Licensing surely is a sensible answer. For what it means is that society should screen out from ownership persons who shouldn't have handguns—perpetrators of violent crime, for example. The trouble with this idea is that most murders are committed by persons who previously had no felony record against them. They merely pick up and use a weapon that is available to them in a moment of passion. So screening out the felons isn't the complete answer, although it would do some good.

If pistols and revolvers were eliminated from the general public, society would be dealing with the major murder weapon. Because the handgun is *concealable*, it is the weapon of crime; because it is *available*, it is the instrument used in suicide and crimes of passion. Banning handguns nationally would greatly reduce the number of gun killings in the United States. Such a law could be evenly and simply administered. Unlike many other gun control laws, it would be very difficult to circumvent.

A handgun law would ban handguns from importation, manufacture, sale, possession, and use by the general American public. There would be reasonable exceptions: the military, the police, security officers, and pistol clubs—where guns would be kept on the premises under secure conditions. Gun dealers would also be permitted to trade in antique weapons kept and sold in unfireable condition. Similar legislation has been introduced into each new Congress for many years.

In 1975 the Gallup poll showed that 41 percent of the American people favor banning handguns. A poll by CBS in 1976 reflected that that number had increased to 51 percent. When the figure rises to about 70 percent, then the mores of the American people will be sufficient to support a law that could be successfully enforced. Only then shall we move toward a less violent and more civilized society.

III. LEGISLATION

EDITOR'S INTRODUCTION

*A well-regulated militia being necessary to the security
of a free State, the right of the people to keep and bear
arms shall not be infringed.*

This is the second amendment to our Constitution and the
first gun law in a long series of legislation. While the amendment guaranteed the right to carry a gun, our interpretation
of it has changed over the years, allowing for passage of regulation as the need arose. The first two articles in this section
show how difficult it is to pass federal gun legislation. Charles
Orasin, Vice President of Handgun Control, reveals in *USA
Today* how the strong intentions of candidate Carter were
frustrated after he took office by pro-gun lobbies, including
the NRA, and the "militant minority." In "A Failure of
Nerve," Peter Stuart, a reporter for the *Christian Science
Monitor,* maintains that only an emergency, such as another
assassination, and the resultant public outcry can counteract
that "high-powered gun lobby" in the Congress.

The Federal Gun Control Act of 1968 is discussed in the
third article, which is written by M. Stanton Evans and reprinted from the *National Review.* Hastily enacted in response to the Kennedy and King assassinations, the law is
"weak and flawed," according to Mr. Evans. Restricting the
sale, collection, and use of guns, it was found to be riddled
with loopholes and open to abuses by the Bureau of Alcohol,
Tobacco and Firearms (BATF), the enforcing authority. The
McClure-Volkmer bill, if passed by Congress, would be a step
toward strengthening the existing law and closing up the
loopholes. In the fourth article, "Washington Report," which
is reprinted from *Guns and Ammo,* Jim Oliver, reporter,

documents some of the specific complaints about the 1968 Act by the National Rifle Association Institute for Legislative Action and discusses the withdrawal of the BATF proposal to create a national computerized records system on gun transactions.

Below the federal level, a number of states have attempted to pass effective gun legislation. Lawrence O'Toole, the author of the next two articles in this section, both reprinted from *MacLean's*, writes on illegal handguns in New York, where Mayor Koch's demand for mandatory sentencing of Sullivan Law violators has met with heavy opposition from rifle groups and Republican legislators. The final article is an analysis of the New York Gun Law of 1980 which requires mandatory sentencing with exceptions.

HANDGUN CONTROL AND THE POLITICS OF FEAR[1]

During his campaign for the Presidency, Jimmy Carter took a stand which, in the eyes of some, seemed a bit surprising for a Southern governor from a rural area. He firmly and forcefully endorsed the need for effective handgun control legislation in the U.S.

Initially, candidate Carter made the statement as part of a fund-raising appeal to the public. He was seeking special funds in order to beat George Wallace in the Florida primary. In his letter, Carter said: "You and I will agree on some issues, disagree on others. I favor handgun control."

As his campaign progressed, Carter clarified his position and added it to his growing list of campaign promises—to be kept when elected. He said: "I favor registration of handguns, a ban on the sale of cheap handguns, reasonable licensing provisions including a waiting period, and a prohibition of

[1] Article by Charles J. Orasin, Executive Vice President, Handgun Control Inc. *USA Today.* 108:8. Ja. '80. Copyright 1980 by Society for the Advancement of Education. Reprinted from *USA Today*, January 1980.

ownership by anyone convicted of a crime involving a gun, and by those not mentally competent."

Not unexpectedly, Carter's position brought forth the wrath of that militant minority of Americans who not only oppose any new handgun control legislation, but are seeking to repeal existing laws on the books. The National Rifle Association endorsed the candidacy of Gerald Ford for president and sent out mailings to its members urging them to re-elect Ford. This unprecedented effort may have cost Carter the votes of a fervent few who are gun fanatics, but his stand also won him the support of millions of other Americans, who shared his handgun control convictions and respected his courage. These voters believed that Jimmy Carter—Southerner, small-town businessman, fiscal conservative, Naval Academy graduate, military man, hunter, and sportsman—was uniquely qualified to lead and educate the American people on the issue of handgun control. The last president to really push for national law was Lyndon Johnson—a Texan.

Shortly after the 1976 elections, handgun control supporters became convinced that their hopes had been well placed. Hamilton Jordan, the President's chief political advisor, wrote: "I am sure that you will find that the Administration's efforts in the area of gun control will move in the direction in which your organization advocates." Testifying before the Senate Judiciary Committee, Attorney General Griffin Bell told Senator Edward Kennedy: "It is past time for handgun control."

This warm reception to the views of handgun control supporters encouraged activists to continue the dialogue. Meetings were held with the key principals at the Department of Justice who were charged with drafting the President's handgun control bill. The outcome was comprehensive legislation to stem the epidemic of handgun violence in America, which was sent to the White House in June, 1977. Then, however, something happened—something called fear, a very special kind of fear. It is not the kind of fear that millions of Americans feel—fear for their safety on the streets, in businesses, in homes because of handguns. It is not the fear a mother or father feels after their son has been critically wounded by a handgun. No, it was not that kind of fear.

What the Carter Administration felt, and what Congress has felt, is a different kind of fear—political fear. Jimmy Carter's advisors and strategists are afraid of the militant minority of Americans who will stop at nothing in their misguided efforts to stop handgun control.

These Carter advisors will tell you that the pro-gun minority cuts across the traditional political, economic, and geographical lines. They will tell you that, in 1978, these single-issue gun lovers were instrumental in defeating Senators and Congressmen for office. They will tell you that the gun forces are able to raise millions of dollars and funnel hundreds of thousands of dollars directly into the campaign chests of pro-gun office-seekers. Most important, Carter's aides will tell you that the majority of Americans who favor handgun control really don't give a damn at the ballot box. Their minds are on pocketbook issues and not guns. For these voters, handgun control is not a crucial issue.

These conclusions have led Carter strategists to decide the best political approach is to sit tight and do nothing about any handgun control legislation on Capitol Hill. That way, they believe, they can keep the militant minority appeased, while providing the handgun control forces with empty promises for action "some time in the future." It is a strategy to soothe everyone—everyone, that is, except the 30 Americans who will be robbed or assaulted with a handgun during the next 60 minutes; everyone except the 24 Americans who will be murdered with handguns during the next 24 hours; everyone except those Americans who give a damn; everyone except those Americans who want to put a stop to this handgun madness.

Handgun control advocates are now making it a point to remind the American public what candidate Carter said on handgun control and what President Carter ... [was] doing. The increased focus on the handgun issue in the press led to a direct question to the President at an April, 1979, news conference. The President was asked about his long-delayed handgun control bill and if he would send it to the Congress. President Carter said: "I think to pursue it aggressively in the Congress would be a mistake. . . ."

This statement by the President indicated a total abandonment of his handgun control legislation. Handgun control advocates are now in a position of looking for new leadership on the handgun control issue. The only American political leader who possesses the political clout to win passage of legislation is Senator Edward Kennedy. As the result of retirements, Senator Kennedy . . . [was] chairman of the powerful Senate Judiciary Committee . . . leading the fight for handgun control not only in the Senate, but in the public eye. As one who lost two brothers to assassination, he can readily appreciate the suffering of the tens of thousands of American families who have lost loved ones.

Congress and the Gun Lobby

Even with Senator Kennedy's leadership, however, an intense and difficult legislative fight lies ahead. The political fear the President . . . [felt] had its origin in the Congress. Its history is fairly recent. In 1970, Senator Joseph Tydings (D.-Md.), author of handgun control proposals, ran for reelection. The gun lobby listed him as target number one for the 1970 elections. When he lost by a slim margin of two percent, the gun lobby claimed credit. However, most political observers believe that a series of Nixon "dirty tricks," including a *Life Magazine* article accusing Tydings of using influence to help a company of which he was a shareholder, were the real reasons for the loss.

Despite no real evidence that the gun lobby had been the difference, the word spread on Capitol Hill that the gun forces now had political muscle. Whenever a legislative proposal came before the Congress, the gun lobby would orchestrate massive mailings of letters and postcards. The word behind each of these communications was "vote." In other words, the Congressman should recognize that these letterwriters were potential votes against him if the legislator failed to vote the proper way. When a legislator receives thousands and thousands of pro-gun constituent letters, he listens, especially if he won his seat in the Congress by a slim margin.

Within recent years, the gun lobby has fine-tuned the art of political intimidation. In 1976, the National Rifle Association (NRA) publicly announced the formation of its "Political Victory Fund." Its purpose is, in the words of the NRA, "to work for the defeat of anti-gun candidates and for support and election of pro-gun office-seekers." The NRA called its new effort "a gloves-off political operation." It said, "this action can spell the difference on Capitol Hill." The NRA political group and a few other gun political action committees spent over $200,000 in 1976, which was the year a handgun control bill—the first since 1968—passed the House Judiciary Committee. Obviously, the NRA and its allies felt it was time to reestablish itself as a political entity.

Senator Kennedy recently said:

Representative government on Capitol Hill is in the worst shape I have seen it in my 16 years in the Senate. The heart of the problem is that the Senate and the House are awash in a sea of special interest campaign contributions and special interest lobbying.

Nowhere is the truth of that statement more evident than when it comes to the issue of handgun control. In 1978, an unprecedented amount of money was spent by the pro-gun forces to elect and defeat candidates for public office. The NRA Political Victory Fund raised over $600,000 and spent nearly $550,000. The Gun Owners of America Campaign Committee, another pro-gun committee, amassed nearly $700,000 and spent over $600,000. Hundreds of thousands of dollars were funnelled into the campaign chests of pro-gun office-seekers. Thousands of other dollars were used to organize gun supporters in selected Congressional districts and get them to the polls. When the votes were finally tallied in November, the NRA alone claimed to have beaten Rep. Donald Fraser (D.-Minn.) and Senators Dick Clark (D.-Iowa),

William Hathaway (D.-Maine), and Thomas McIntyre (D.-
N.H.) by using its political cash.

The political pundits, in their analysis of the 1978 elections, again pointed to other reasons for the defeat of handgun
control advocates. They have cited the abortion issue, lower
voter turn-out, miscalculations by incumbents, etc. However,
the fact remains that this demonstration of political clout
makes the Congress stand up and take notice. It is the carrot-
stick approach. The politician who follows the direction of
the gun lobby is rewarded with a political contribution. With
the high cost of election campaigns, every dollar is welcome.
There are Congressmen and Senators willing to fight for the
cause of handgun control. The NRA targets them for defeat
and seeks out candidates to replace them. If the NRA is successful, they maintain their good relationship with the new
Congressman and assist in his reelection.

Thus, despite the fact that a 1978 Harris survey showed
that over 80 percent of the American people—including gun
owners—favor handgun control legislation, the Congress and
the President will not act. The gun lobby's bullying, bad-
gering, and buying of Congress has worked. The President's
advisors, knowing of the gun lobby's efforts against the Congress, . . . [were] wary of kicking into gear any pro-gun political effort aimed at the presidential election of 1980.

What Can Be Done?

Congress fears and the President fears. Meanwhile, in the
time it has taken to read this article this far, another American has been assaulted with one of the nearly 50,000,000
handguns out there. What can be done against this powerful,
wealthy force?

The secret of the gun lobby's strength is the intensity of its
members. Although the National Rifle Association claims
over 1,000,000 members, it is safe to guess that only about
one-third are really hard-core gun fanatics. These are the
members the NRA draws upon for letters to the Congress, for
lobbying money, and for political activity.

The gun lobby is effective in distorting information and misrepresenting facts to its constituency. Every piece of sound legislation is portrayed to the gun membership in its worst possible evolution. The base message is that the government is after their guns and only the gun lobby can stop it.

Using "fear" words such as "confiscation," "communism," "criminal," and "constitutional right," the gun lobby hypes its intense membership to a frenzy. This leads to a tremendous outpouring of money into the gun war-chests for both lobbying and political action. Having practiced this technique year after year unchallenged, the gun lobby has been able to assume leverage totally out of proportion to the numbers it actually represents. Yet, this leverage has proven successful in stopping every legislative initiative.

Congress and the President will only understand how deeply the American people feel about the threat of handgun violence when the majority of Americans exert counter-political pressure to the gun lobby. Congress and the President will only act when they recognize that their political lives are on the line if they don't pass a handgun control law. Until that day, a new handgun will be sold every 13 seconds, and the chance of becoming a victim of handgun violence will increase.

The intensity of the gun owner who fears the loss of a piece of cold metal can easily be matched by the intensity of a handgun victim who has lost a loved one because of handgun violence. By telling, retelling, and retelling again his encounter with handgun violence to the public, a victim can explain why the unaffected American should act now to prevent handgun violence from striking him.

There will be at least 250,000 more victims of handgun crime in America one year from now. Millions have already suffered from the scourge of these easily concealable weapons. By this time tomorrow, 24 more Americans will be murdered by handguns. Someone is robbed with a handgun every two minutes.

Some 50,000,000 uncontrolled handguns are currently in circulation in the U.S. Each year, over 2,000,000 more hand-

guns are sold into civilian hands. At the current rate of production and importation, there will be some 100,000,000 uncontrolled handguns in private hands by the year 2000. The
U.S. is the *only* civilized nation without effective handgun
curbs.

As the stories of handgun victims and the horrible statistics are brought to the attention of the American people, they
will begin to respond. Still, for the majority of Americans who
vote, single-issue politics is not acceptable. For them, the
handgun issue might be listed among such other concerns as
inflation, energy, etc. The intense single-issue voters, however, can be found among the victims of handgun crime and
the young who are just entering the adult society.

Victims of handgun violence would vote out a pro-gun
Congressman because of their first-hand knowledge of handgun violence. The young voters must be shown the handgun
danger ahead in their lives. The majority of them, unfortunately, don't believe their vote means a damn; they feel they
have no political clout. However, they can demonstrate effectively that they do have clout by systematically organizing. A
decade ago, their older brothers and sisters opened America's
eyes to the horror of Vietnam. Today, the youth can open
America's eyes to the horror of handgun violence.

During the peak years of the Vietnam War, more Americans were murdered here at home with handguns than
American soldiers were killed in combat. Young people
"feared" that their number might come up in the draft lottery
and that they might face death, so they sought to end the war.
Here in America, the handgun war continues unabated.
Young people should "fear" that their number may come
up—while they're crossing the campus, walking downtown,
or jogging through a park. While in school, they have the
time, the idealism, and the energy to shape the society of
their future. They have yet to use their most potent
weapon—the power to vote—in an organized fashion. The
cause of handgun control provides them an opportunity and a
challenge.

A FAILURE OF NERVE[2]

Anyone standing vigil these past ten years on the grassy knoll of Arlington National Cemetery where Robert F. Kennedy lies buried would have gazed across the Potomac upon a capital presiding over dizzying national change. He would have watched the United States end 15 years of war in Southeast Asia and 23 years of isolation from China; give birth to the environmental and women's rights movements; hound a President for the first time into resignation, then defeat his replacement at the polls; demythologize the FBI and CIA; and impose a new standard of political ethics.

Yet the country that has wrought these fundamental accomplishments has been stymied by a relatively uncomplicated problem of particularly painful interest on this Arlington cemetery slope: the private handgun. For since the Senator, former U.S. Attorney General and brother of the assassinated President John F. Kennedy was gunned down on June 4, 1968 by a snub-nosed .22 caliber Iver Johnson Cadet pistol, 120,000 other Americans have been killed by handguns—twice the nation's death toll during half again as many years of organized shooting in Indochina.

Although a weak and flawed gun-control bill cleared the House of Representatives on the day Robert Kennedy died, and later became law, Congress has subsequently rejected handgun registration, either in committee rooms or the chamber of one house or the other, no fewer than 16 times. If not understandable, this masochistic failure is at least explainable. The legislation that was passed made a stab at policing two of the shadier corners of the gun market—mail-order weapons and cheap, concealable "Saturday Night Specials"

[2] Article entitled "A Failure of Nerve; Shooting Down Gun Control," by Peter C. Stuart, reporter from Washington, D.C. for the *Christian Science Monitor*. *The New Leader*. 61:7-9. S. 11, '78. Reprinted with permission from *The New Leader*, September 11, 1978. Copyright 1978 by the American Labor Conference on International Affairs, Inc.

manufactured abroad. It dealt with nothing more, but soaked up the public outrage unleashed by the murders of the Senator and, just two months earlier, the Reverend Martin Luther King Jr. Americans were deluded into believing that they finally had an effective antidote to the madness.

The Republican presidents who occupied the White House for the next eight years showed no interest in genuine gun control. Even after escaping two close-range assassination attempts with handguns just 17 days apart in 1975, Gerald R. Ford, displaying greater personal than political courage, was out on the hustings a year later insisting that "the law-abiding citizens of this country should not be deprived of the right to have firearms in their possession."

The man the voters ultimately elected, though, was the lone contender in an originally large field to espouse curbs gun-control advocates regarded as meaningful. Thus there was reason to think things would be different by the tenth anniversary of Robert Kennedy's slaying.

A position paper cranked out during Carter's campaign put him on record as favoring "registration of handguns, a ban on the sale of cheap handguns, reasonable licensing provisions including a waiting period, and prohibition of ownership by anyone convicted of a crime involving a gun and by those not mentally competent." Only unlikely candidate Fred R. Harris, the former Democratic Senator from Oklahoma, had taken anywhere near as hard a line. Carter's stance made him the most outspokenly pro-gun-control Chief Executive since Lyndon B. Johnson, and statements by his closest associates suggested that the President meant every word of what he said.

The President's Georgian friend and choice for attorney general, Griffin B. Bell, was drawn out on the subject at his confirmation hearings by Senator Edward M. Kennedy (D.-Mass.). Judge Bell allowed as how "I have long thought we ought to have handgun control as distinguished from sportsmen's weapons. We do not seem to be making as much progress in that area as we should. . . . I think we are past time having a handgun control." Top Presidential Assistant Hamilton Jordan was still blunter in a comment to a writer for *New Times* Magazine: "Carter will really go on gun control and really be tough."

In addition, what had once been scorned by House Crime Subcommittee Chairman John Conyers Jr. (D.-Mich.) as "the invisible lobby" started to show surprising strength. The period corresponding roughly to the campaign had seen no fewer than three new national gun-control groups spring up, each with impressive leadership and backing.

One, the National Council to Control Handguns, was launched by a savvy DuPont executive whose son had been a victim of the random shooting by the "Zebra killers" in California; it was quickly to become the most visible anti-gun outfit. Another, the National Coalition to Ban Handguns, embraced 28 religious, educational, labor, and public-service groups. The third, the National Gun Control Center, was the brainchild of Morris Dees, candidate Carter's national finance director, and Joseph J. Levin Jr., who later became a transition-team liaison at the Justice Department.

The high-powered gun lobby, meanwhile, has been engaged in an unusual round of sniping within its own ranks. One hundred and seven years of shooting down attempts at handgun control with a lethal combination of mailbags of angry letters and veiled political threats had given the National Rifle Association (NRA) the image of a smooth-running, well-disciplined fighting machine. Outsiders—as well as many of its own 1 million members—were therefore startled when the presumably monolithic NRA last year was shaken by a coup. Dissidents, apparently angered by plans to move the organization's headquarters from downtown Washington to pristine Colorado Springs, Colorado, ousted the leadership for, of all things, not being militant enough.

The NRA has also had to cope with an external challenge from some of its allies. For as long as anyone can remember, the "gun lobby" has meant the NRA; the two terms have been practically synonymous. But the swift rise of several up-

start gun-owner groups associated with the ultra-conservative
political movement known as the "New Right" has relegated
the NRA to the "Old Right."

The competition has been extravagant, and occasionally
nasty. Cashing in on the computerized mailing lists of conservative donors compiled by Richard A. Viguerie, former fund-
raiser for Alabama's Governor George C. Wallace, the Citizens Committee for the Right to Keep and Bear Arms
reported spending three times more money to lobby Congress
in the first quarter of 1978 than did the NRA ($150,050 to
$44,710). A second rival, the Gun Owners of America, nearly
matched the NRA with $39,872. Finding itself in the ironic
position of being out-NRAed, the association is retaliating by
taking pot-shots at its new competitors through its publications. The Citizens Committee, for its part, brashly bills itself
as the "real gun lobby."

Whatever the case, with the anti-gun forces seemingly
flourishing and the pro-gun lobby busy bickering, the Carter
Administration last autumn drafted a handgun bill for Congress. Justice Department and White House officials worked
closely with gun-control leaders from the start, consulting
their opposition counterparts almost as an afterthought, and
the resulting proposal reflected this: It would outlaw the production and sale of new Saturday Night Specials as well as the
transfer of existing ones; impose a three-week waiting period
in handgun purchases for police checks of the buyers; and
hike dealer license fees from the present $10 to $500 to weed
out marginal operators.

"Excellent," exulted gun-controllers. "Repressive," re-
torted gun owners, who this time appeared headed for defeat
or at the very least a tough battle.

Then, almost inexplicably, the cocksure attitude that had
marked the beginning of the administration's pursuit of gun
control suddenly turned into timidity. The proposed legislation, ready to go to Capitol Hill since late . . . [1977], has
never left the White House—and it . . . [didn't in 1978] because of fears of saddling Democrats with a controversial

issue in the upcoming Congressional elections. "I doubt that we'll do anything this year," the domestic policy staffer handling the matter, Annie Gutierrez, conceded to me as the legislative session entered its summer homestretch.

At the same time, the gun-control lobby started losing some of its momentum. The group with the closest ties to the White House, the National Gun Control Center, was absorbed by another organization. The church-based National Coalition to Ban Handguns lost the valuable Federal tax exemption entitling it, as an "educational" group, to tax-deductible contributions. And the U.S. Conference of Mayors was beset by an internal attempt to rescind its handgun-control policy and program.

What really underlies the absence of an effective national handgun control law for yet another year, however, is a failing that goes beyond the White House's loss of courage or the gun-control movement's internal setbacks: Neither the Carter Administration nor the professional gun-controllers have been able to mobilize the consistent public opinion majority in favor of handgun curbs—a steady 65-75 percent margin for gun registration according to a variety of polls over the past decade—into practical political support for legislation.

In the vast stillness left by this silent majority, the almost fanatical fury of those Americans who own handguns (at most, one in five) rings loudly indeed. The NRA has boasted, with some justification, that it can besiege a President or Congress with half a million letters on 72 hours' notice.

Gun-control advocates also have been unable to sell their cause as the crime-fighting device which, stripped of its emotionalism, it basically is. A crime involving a gun occurs somewhere in the United States every two minutes, a handgun death every hour. It is barely publicized, but law-enforcement groups are among the oldest supporters of gun control laws.

Because the crime aspect is poorly perceived, gun control is debated as a "rights" issue. Organized gun owners claim a constitutional right "to keep and bear arms," a phrase from the Second Amendment that has been incorporated into the name of the new organization outstripping the NRA's lobbying efforts.

It is a phony issue, since the U.S. Supreme Court (in a 1939 case, *U.S. v. Miller*) has interpreted the Second Amendment as applying to the legality of states operating National Guard units. Yet in our rights-conscious nation—Americans have been proclaiming their rights from the colonial era's "inalienable Rights" to today's civil rights, women's rights, and gay rights—the arms "right" prevails. Even such thoughtful Western liberals as Senator Frank Church (D.-Idaho) Representative Morris K. Udall (D.-Ariz.) and Representative Thomas S. Foley (D.-Wash.) oppose handgun controls, probably because polls show that support for them is weakest in the West.

The political impotence of gun-control partisans was graphically demonstrated in the recent congressional skirmish over a set of modest regulations proposed by the Treasury Department's Bureau of Alcohol, Tobacco, and Firearms. The regulations would merely have required serial numbers to be stamped on newly manufactured handguns and tighter reporting of gun transactions, to help trace the lost and stolen weapons so often used in crime. But after a withering gun-lobby counterattack, including a fusillade of 300,000 letters from the NRA, the regulations mustered just 80 defenders in the 435-member House of Representatives.

That vote—a nadir for the gun-control movement in a year of once-soaring ambitions—occurred on the day after the 10th anniversary of Robert Kennedy's handgun assassination. "The only thing that may get us another gun-control law," says a procontrol lobbyist, despairingly, "is another assassination."

CRIME AND GUN CONTROL[3]

Eleven years ago, in a reflexive effort to "do something" about the murders of Martin Luther King and Robert Kennedy, Congress passed the Gun Control Act of 1968. It was a fairly typical instance of federal policy-making under stress—with results that could have been, and were, predicted.

The object of the gun law was to cut down on violent crime committed with firearms, and to this end it imposed a host of restrictions on the sale, collection, and use of guns and ammunition. In addition, it conferred extensive powers of enforcement on the Bureau of Alcohol, Tobacco, and Firearms (BATF) of the Department of the Treasury—previously best known for its attempts to crack down on the illicit production and sale of "moonshine" liquor.

To the surprise of virtually no one who has studied such matters, the Gun Control Act has done little to impede the growth of crime in our society. All the indices of criminal activity—including armed robbery, assault, and homicide—continued moving upward at their accustomed giddy rate through the middle 1970s, with no evidence that the '68 law had affected the problem in any way whatever. All of which suggests, to those who favor gun control, that the law didn't go nearly far enough, and that other, more stringent, gun laws are needed in its stead.

A number of congressmen and senators, however, have come up with a different reading of the subject. They note that, while the '68 law has done nothing to alter behavior patterns among the criminal element, it has done a great deal to infringe the liberties of the law-abiding. In particular, they charge, the law has been used to harass citizens engaged in the perfectly innocent sale and collection of guns, and has

[3] Article by M. Stanton Evans, syndicated columnist, Los Angeles *Times*. *National Review*. 31:1434. N. 9, '79. Copyright 1979 by National Review Inc. Reprinted with permission.

given BATF inordinate power to enforce unreasonable regulations on people who have not committed any sort of crime.

A number of examples are pointed out by Senator James McClure (R.–Idaho) and Representative Harold Volkmer (D.–Mo.). They note that, under the existing gun law, there is no clear definition of what constitutes "engaging in the business" of selling firearms and ammunition—and charge that BATF refuses to provide one. As a result, a given individual may be (1) denied a dealer's license on the grounds that his level of transactions is too small to constitute a business; and (2) cited by BATF thereafter for doing business without a license.

McClure and Volkmer cite numerous other such examples under the existing law: searches and seizures without sufficient probable cause, seizure of firearms that have nothing to do with any alleged criminal violation, onerous record-keeping requirements, enforcement of regulations that were never intended by Congress, etc. The net effect, they charge, is to constrict the freedom of the law-abiding citizen, while doing nothing to slow the incidence of crime. These lawmakers have accordingly proposed a comprehensive bill to right the situation—the Federal Firearms Law Reform Act of 1979.

Stricter Guidelines

McClure is the principal sponsor of this legislation in the upper chamber (S-1862), where it has quickly obtained some 31 co-sponsors, ranging from Mark Hatfield (R.–Ore.) and Warren Magnuson (D.–Wash.) on the Left, to Barry Goldwater (R.–Ariz.) and Strom Thurmond (R.–S.C.) on the Right. Joining Volkmer as co-sponsors in the House (HR-5225) are Representatives Michael Synar (D.–Okla.), John Ashbrook (R.–Ohio), James Sensenbrenner (R.–Wis.), Robert Bauman (R.–Md.), and 25 other congressmen.

In form, the McClure-Volkmer bill is a series of amendments to the 1968 law. It seeks to straighten out the definitional ambiguities of the 1968 act, lay down stricter guidelines for BATF enforcement acitivities, and overturn specific

measures the agency has taken which, in the view of the legislators, violate the intent of Congress and/or the liberties of
the citizen. The effect would be to leave the basic elements of
the gun law in place, but to eliminate the loopholes for abuse.

Punishing Criminals

Among other features, the McClure-Volkmer legislation
would (1) establish clear standards for determining who is
"engaging in the business" of dealing in firearms; (2) require
BATF to have reasonable grounds for believing a violation of
the law to have occurred before entering and inspecting the
premises of a licensee; (3) establish a "legislative veto" procedure for BATF regulations concerning firearms, and, specifically, nullify a rule concerning the sale of powder, assertedly
contrary to the original will of Congress; (4) create a uniform
standard for sales to out-of-state residents—an activity that is
currently subject to immense confusion.

Also, the reform bill seeks to strengthen existing law in the
other direction, beefing up the mandatory sentencing provisions for crimes committed with a firearm. Under McClure-
Volkmer, a defendant committing a second violent offense involving a gun would be ineligible for probation or parole
until his minimum sentence had been completed. The thrust
of the amendments, in other words, is to minimize harassment
of the average citizen, while tightening penalties on the criminal.

The latter distinction, of course, goes to the heart of the
controversy. Gun control proponents, by and large, are reluc-
tant to hold individual offenders accountable for their behavior—preferring to assign the blame for aberrant conduct to
external factors, in this case the availability of firearms, and
the society which permits them. The forces behind the reform
bill, on the other hand, believe responsibility for criminal behavior should be assessed against the criminal, rather than
being imposed on society at large, or blamed on an inanimate
object. The way to cope with crime, these people argue, is to
punish the guilty. It just might work.

WASHINGTON REPORT[4]

As its major legislative objective for the 96th Congress, the NRA Institute for Legislative Action . . . [was] declaring war on the 1968 Gun Control Act.

In launching what he called "this long-overdue offensive," ILA's Executive Director Neal Knox pledged "every effort, every resource to the task of dismantling the more onerous provisions of the ten-year-old Federal gun law." Knox called the law "a terrible abuse of personal freedom," saying "the enforcement of the law by the Bureau of Alcohol, Tobacco and Firearms has been even worse."

Knox's announcement of the offensive came in a letter mailed to 1.5 million NRA members and supporters of ILA and in a Washington D.C. press conference.

"This is a beginning. From this point we shall work to change the worst sections of the law first. Whittling down this bad law—this clearly evil law—is a long-term effort. It will not be accomplished in just a single session of the Congress. It will prove to be a war of attrition—a long war, but a war that will ultimately be won for and by the nation's 50 million law abiding firearms owners," Knox said.

He said that ILA's effort to expose wide-spread civil rights abuses against gun owners and licensed dealers by agents of the BATF "is integral to our pledge of taking lost ground. If there is a single message in the last ten years under the 1968 Gun Control Act it is that *evil men with evil intent can inflict all manner of abuse under the color of an evil law.'*"

Very clearly that has been the case with the 1968 Gun Control Act—an act which claimed as its purpose the reduction of crime, but which demonstrates in its application, an unparalleled abuse of Federal police powers leveled at an en-

[4] Article by Jim Oliver, *Guns & Ammo.* 23:6. My. '79. Copyright 1979 by Petersen Publishing Company. Reprinted by permission.

tire class of law abiding citizens, at anyone who would lawfully wish to own and use a firearm."

With Congressional hearings sought by ILA on misconduct by the Bureau of Alcohol, Tobacco and Firearms, Knox explained that many of the more onerous provisions of the GCA '68 will be exposed to public view.

"Virtually every abuse which can be documented against BATF demonstrates grievous flaws in the Federal gun control statutes," Knox said. "But at the very heart of the problem is the concept of gun laws—a concept which has proven time and time again to be false. No gun law has ever deterred a criminal. They only deter the rights of innocent citizens."

Specifically, Knox said, the '68 Act has been used by Federal gun control police—the BATF—to create crime where none exists, to entrap innocent citizens into breaking the most minor provisions of the Federal gun law. "All violations of the '68 Act, no matter how minor, are Federal felonies."

In his letter to the NRA membership announcing the campaign to take legislative ground lost in 1968, he cited examples of the inherent dangers of the gun law. "Under the GCA '68, you and I are guilty of violating the law—and face five years imprisonment if we give any gun to a father, mother, son or daughter living in another state. Or if we give some handloaded ammo to a friend."

Knox said the war on the '68 Act "marks a turning point in the history of the National Rifle Association. Always before we have reacted to problems. Now we are strong enough to act; to take back lost ground. So long as we only defended, the gun prohibitionists could fail the proverbial seven times, or seventy times seven. While we could lose but once. We are now taking the fight to our foes, forcing them to spend their strengths, their energies and their money," Knox said.

"Those who devised GCA '68 are again saying we must 'compromise' by giving up handguns, or risk losing our rifles or shotguns. Nuts! That kind of compromise means losing. It means voluntarily giving up more than the antigun forces are big enough to take. The NRA Institute will not compromise," he said, "Except in one area: This year, we will accept repeal of half of the gun control act. That's a reasonable first step toward sensible gun laws."

Knox's declaration is expected to be widely supported in both Houses of Congress, especially by members of the pro-gun leadership who support efforts such as Idaho Senator James A. McClure's bill to completely repeal the '68 Gun Control Act.

As a clear indication of firearms owners' legislative and political clout, the Bureau of Alcohol, Tobacco and Firearms quietly informed the House Appropriations Committee that the BATF proposal to create a national computerized records system on gun transactions has been withdrawn.

The announcement of the withdrawal before the Appropriations Treasury subcommittee was particularly poignant, since that legislative unit, chaired by Oklahoma Representative Tom Steed, had initiated the massive BATF funding cut enacted by Congress last summer.

In the official notice of the regulations withdrawal—published in the *Federal Register*—BATF said that opposition from citizens contributed greatly to the decision.

"ATF received approximately 345,000 comments on these proposals. While support was received from various law enforcement and other organizations, the overwhelming number of comments were negative."

In its *Federal Register* announcement, BATF failed to spell out the magnitude of the opposition, a total 337,000 comments were filed in opposition to the regulations.

In a press conference held jointly by the National Coalition to Ban Handguns, and that group's Congressional stalwarts, Illinois Representative Abner Mikva made the appeal to the President to resurrect his much-touted gun control bill—which was in the last session of Congress, but was never introduced.

Mikva, in the press conference, said nothing new, but reiterated his standard diatribe against handguns. "I would like to see a law banning the manufacture, sale and distribution of all handguns. In my mind a handgun is manufactured for one purpose only, and that's to kill a fellow human being. It's a lousy hunting weapon," he said.

Michael Beard of the Coalition to Ban Handguns, used the press conference to make a startling revelation: "I would agree that no law is going to prevent criminals from getting handguns or any kind of weapon . . . you can't take guns away from criminals."

Beard also said his friends in the Congress would press the BATF for new statistics on handgun ownership. "We don't even have an idea how many guns are out there, and that's an indictment of the whole system as it is now . . . There's no place that particular dangerous weapon is recorded so that we know how many there are in the hands of private citizens," he said. "And that's one of the things the BATF regulations were about." ·

NEW YORK GUN LAW DISPUTE[5]

When two junior-high-school students were arrested in New York recently for robbing a ten-year-old boy, police discovered the thieves had a .22-calibre revolver and a .38-calibre pistol. That incident and many others, abetted by the frightening fact that 13 police officers have been shot dead so far this year in New York's raging handgun war, led to heated exchanges last week in Albany, where hearings were under way on tough new gun laws for the state.

The debating bloods were brought to a boil by a bill proposed by New York City Mayor Edward Koch which provides that anyone found with an illegal handgun or rifle be given a mandatory one-year jail sentence without recourse to plea-bargaining or probation. And backers of the bill cited some staggering figures in its support. While there are an estimated two million illegal handguns in New York City, they pointed

[5] Article entitled "Gunfight at the Not-O.K. Corral," by Lawrence O'Toole, New York columnist. *MacLean's.* 93:29. My. 5, '80. Copyright 1980 MacLean-Hunter.

out, the number seized by police within the past few years has
steadily dropped and there has been an increase in handgun-
related killings of both police and civilians. Equally disturbing, handguns claimed 1,174 lives across the nation during the
first three months of 1980.

Charles Peterson, president of New York City's Patrol-
men's Benevolent Association, argued the policemen's case.
"Please, help us," he said. "We're outnumbered 100 to 1.
We're at war in the city of New York." The police contend
that owning a legal gun doesn't necessarily improve the
chances of surviving a robbery or mugging, that protection
often backfires. Indeed, in a recent case, a Chinese restaura-
teur who fired his gun at a robber fatally wounded his own
13-year-old daughter and, two weeks ago, a Queens restaura-
teur was killed when he drew his licensed gun on two holdup
men. Running scared, the police have already made it difficult to obtain an application, let alone a permit, for a handgun.

On the other hand the senate's Republican faction argued
that gun control is, largely, a New York City problem, and
stressed the average citizen's need for self-protection. Lend-
ing their support were sportsmen and the Federation of New
York State Rifle and Pistol Clubs, who claim existing laws are
adequate. As well, the state correction commissioner testified
that the prisons were already almost full and couldn't accom-
modate ordinarily non-criminal people caught with an illegal
handgun. Chief Administrative Judge Herbert Evans added
that the cost of handling, say, 312 new gun trials annually
would run about $2.8 million.

Koch and the police did have a trump card: a recent study
at Boston's Northeastern University showed significant de-
clines in gun-related crimes and homicides in the city in the
wake of new laws which made jail terms mandatory for carrying an unlicensed gun. But even that carried little weight
with many of the legislators at Albany's Alexander Hamilton
room, named, coincidentally, after a man who was shot to
death in a duel.

NEW YORK'S TOUGH GUN LAW ISN'T[6]

It was 11:40 a.m. Friday, June 13, [1980] when Governor
Hugh Carey signed New York state's long-awaited and controversial handgun bill. In New York City, where there are an
estimated two million illegal handguns, a man was shot with
one of them—just 35 minutes later. That weekend there were
12 shootings involving illegal handguns, including the
wounding of a six-year-old Queens girl picnicking with her
family. New York state's handgun war, which is virtually a
New York City problem, was still being waged as furiously as
ever.

The new bill, which will not be effective until 60 days
after the signing, to allow for administrative changes, was
called "the toughest handgun law in the country" by Carey,
but others aren't so satisfied with it. Under the new law, anyone caught carrying a loaded, unlicensed handgun can be
charged with an "armed" felony, with a mandatory penalty of
a year in prison, and the illegal sale of handguns has been
changed from a misdemeanor to a felony. Illegally owning or
selling more than 20 handguns could result in a 25-year jail
term.

However, the new statute allows anyone indicted for carrying or selling illegal guns the opportunity to request a hearing pleading "mitigating circumstances," and discounts first
offenders carrying an *unloaded* gun. Ultimately, in the case of
plea-hearings, punishment is left to the discretion of judges
empowered to reduce the so-called mandatory sentence. One
New York precinct commander called the new law "a lawyer's bill. It just creates loopholes that the lawyers will be
able to exploit." But New York City Mayor Edward Koch, responsible for spearheading the drive for stricter gun controls,

[6] Article by Lawrence O'Toole, New York columnist. *MacLean's*. 93:11. Jl. 21, '80.
Copyright 1980 MacLean-Hunter.

described it as "a significant first step in the fight to remove illegal handguns from the streets of our city," and added that he might seek additional legislation if necessary. Variously described by some officials as "half a loaf" and "better than what we have now," the "toughest gun law in the country" generated gratitude from others who felt it nothing short of amazing that the legislature, a number of whom own guns and advocate their use, passed the bill at all.

IV. ENFORCEMENT

EDITOR'S INTRODUCTION

The effectiveness of gun control laws in the United States depends to a large extent on how well governments enforce them, which is a matter not only of justice but also of economics. In the process of enforcement, there is the danger that heavy police measures might produce civil rights violations, while on the other hand, inconsistent and sporadic enforcement might render the legislation ineffective, as in the cases of the Prohibition and marijuana laws. The first article, reprinted from the *Criminal Law Bulletin*, is a study of the effects of the moderately successful Massachusetts mandatory minimum sentence gun law. David Rossman and associates compare police action in gun-possession cases both before and after the passage of the Bentley-Fox Law of 1974. Its sponsor, Judge J. John Fox, regards it as "a finger in the dike against the wave of violence."

The second article, "Gun Laws and Gun Collectors," is by David Hardy, lawyer for the NRA Legislative Action Committee. He discusses the effects of the Federal Gun Control Act of 1968 on the gun dealer and relates incidents in which enforcement of the law by the Bureau of Alcohol, Tobacco and Firearms could be characterized by confiscation, vindictiveness and entrapment. In the next article, reprinted from the *Washingtonian Magazine*, author Joseph Goulden selects a specific case, that of gun dealer Richard Boulin, to demonstrate such victimization at federal hands under the law.

The writers in the final two articles take the position that the cost of gun laws far outweighs the benefits. Writing in

Criminal Law Bulletin, Raymond Kessler, a sociologist, states
that using criminal sanctions to deal with what is essentially a
social problem has definite negative effects. He points out
that enforcement of laws against so-called victimless crime,
such as the 1968 Act, involves prohibitive police and court
costs, not to mention the potential for police corruption and
criminal profits from illegal sales. In an article reprinted from
Harper's, Don Kates Jr. makes the case that as a society we
cannot afford to build enough jail cells for all the violators of
gun control laws. Moreover, such legislation could only succeed in mainly taking guns away from law-abiding citizens
seeking protection, not from criminals. He makes a plea for
institutional and cultural changes instead of a spate of legislation.

MASSACHUSETTS GUN LAW[1]

On June 3, 1974, a bill known as the Bartley-Fox law was
introduced in both houses of the Massachusetts General
Court. It was the end of a legislative session marked by virulent debate over the issues of gun control, registration, and
confiscation. The new statutory proposal dealt with this general issue by changing the criminal sentence for the offense of
carrying a firearm without proper authorization. The Bartley-Fox law preserved the general structure of the Massachusetts gun control statutes, adding only a mandatory minimum
one-year sentence for those convicted of illegally carrying a
firearm. The new law also prohibited suspended sentences,
probation, and various informal means of avoiding sentencing

[1] Article entitled "Massachusetts Mandatory Minimum Sentence Gun Law: Enforcement, Prosecution, and Defense Impact," by David Rossman, Director of Clinical
Programs in Criminal Law at Boston University School of Law, and Paul Froyd, Boston
University School of Law, Glen L. Pierce and John McDevitt and William J. Bowers
from Northeastern University. *Criminal Law Bulletin.* 16:150+. Mr.-Ap. '80. Copyright
1980 by Warren, Gorham & Lamont, Inc., 210 South Street, Boston 02111. Reprinted
by permission.

a defendant whom the prosecution has shown to have violated the gun-carrying prohibition. Passed almost unanimously by both houses, the bill was signed into law on July 30, 1974, and went into final effect on April 1, 1975.

The bill's co-author, retired Judge J. John Fox, called the new law "a finger in the dike against the wave of violence." By removing judicial discretion in the sentencing process, Fox expected the law to be a precedent for altering patterns of judicial behavior and ending the drift he perceived toward lenient sentences for all crimes of violence. In his words: "This bill is aimed to change people's thinking . . . to make people understand that there are laws and there is punishment."

Indeed, the statement of legislative purpose and intent issued shortly after the amendment was passed in both houses takes Fox's reasoning explicitly into account.

The General Court finds that a major source of violent crime in the Commonwealth is the permissive attitude of the society in general and law enforcement agencies, including courts, in particular, toward the unlicensed carrying of firearms, rifles and shotguns by persons away from their home and places of legitimate business. The purpose and intent of this legislation is to impose a one-year mandatory jail sentence without exception for any person female or male who is unlicensed to carry a firearm away from her or his home or place of business.

Seen from this perspective, the amendment is not merely stricter gun control. Sponsored during an election year, the bill was introduced as a measure to "make it safe for the law-abiding citizen to work, move about safely, and enjoy his family and friends and the fruits of his labor." Offered as a tough law-and-order measure, the bill quickly won the approval of traditional gun control opponents.

The Bartley-Fox law was at the forefront of an emerging national interest in mandatory sentencing. It has several implications for the Commonwealth of Massachusetts. Since the law had as its focus the illegal use of firearms, one important measure of its effect is on the crime rate. Did the law affect assaults, robberies, and homicides? Another area of the law's

124 **The Reference Shelf**

impact was on the Massachusetts criminal justice system and how it would adapt to a mandatory sentencing scheme. Would police officers arrest suspects for illegally carrying a firearm at the same rate? Would defendants arrested for illegal gun carrying be charged with a different crime in order to avoid the mandatory minimum sentence? Would plea bargaining go on in Bartley-Fox cases? Would gun-carrying defendants be convicted or go to jail at the same rate as before Bartley-Fox?

In order to answer these questions, the Law Enforcement Assistance Administration of the United States Department of Justice awarded a grant to the Boston University Center for Criminal Justice to conduct a two-year study of the effects of the Bartley-Fox law. The Center for Criminal Justice was aided in its effort by the Center for Applied Social Research of Northeastern University. This LEAA study followed an initial investigation of Bartley-Fox by researchers from Harvard University (See Beha, "*And Nobody Can Get You Out*") who examined the effect of the law after its first year. The current report relied in part on data from the Harvard researchers, but in order to provide a more complete picture of the law's impact, we collected a wider range of data over a longer period of time.

This report relied upon crime statistics from both the FBI and the Boston Police Department; arrest reports from the Boston Police Department; court records from Boston, Worcester, and Springfield; and interviews with criminal justice personnel—judges, defense attorneys, prosecutors, police officers, as well as inmates—throughout the state. Although the report draws conclusions about the effect of Bartley-Fox on crime rates in Massachusetts and on the criminal justice system in these cities (Boston, Worcester, and Springfield), the focus for most of the discussion is the state's largest city, Boston.

A summary of the major findings of this report ... [follows]:

Bartley-Fox and the Crime Rate

Since the Bartley-Fox law was intended to convey to the public a "get tough" message on crime, one important area in which to explore the effect of the law was on the crime rate. We looked at the impact of Bartley-Fox on the crime rate in Boston, for the rest of the state, and for the state as a whole for three types of crime: armed assault, armed robbery, and homicide. In each area, we found that the introduction of the Bartley-Fox law did have an impact on the crime rate.

Armed Assault Rate. Introduction of the Bartley-Fox law had an immediate two-fold effect on armed assault in Massachusetts. First, the law substantially reduced the actual incidence of gun assaults even before its effective date in Massachusetts. Second, after the law went into effect, non-gun assaults in Massachusetts substantially increased. Indeed, there was a statistically significant increase throughout the state in non-gun armed assaults shortly after the Bartley-Fox law went into effect and within a couple of months of the earlier statistically significant decrease in gun assaults. Thus, although the law discouraged gun-related assaults, it probably encouraged non-gun armed assaults, perhaps because it did not keep offenders away from assaultive situations.

The introduction of the Bartley-Fox law also probably had the unanticipated effect of stretching the crime-reporting behavior of citizens. Specifically, citizens were more likely to report less serious forms of gun assaults to the police after implementation of the gun law. This trend was most pronounced in Boston, and it tended to obscure the magnitude of the law's deterrent effects.

Armed Robbery Rate. Our analysis indicates that the gun law had a moderate deterrent effect on gun robberies in 1975 in Boston and, to a lesser extent, in the rest of the state. In 1976, the estimated deterrent effect of the law was much more pronounced and was of approximately equal magnitude in Boston and non-Boston Massachusetts. The displacement effects of the Bartley-Fox law on non-gun armed robbery are less consistent and less pronounced than in the case of non-gun armed assaults.

In contrast to the assault findings, we observed in Boston by 1977 the beginning of a shift back to the use of guns in street, taxi, and residential robberies. This upturn in gun robberies points to the need for analysis over a longer potential-impact period. It is crucial to see whether this tendency for guns to return in armed robbery will continue until the pre-Bartley-Fox level is achieved, or whether it will stabilize short of that level.

Homicide Rate. Due to data limitations, the analysis of criminal homicides was restricted to Boston and its control jurisdictions. The results of the analysis showed evidence of a deterrent effect of the law on gun homicides, but no indication of displacement effects on nongun homicides. Further refinements of the homicide analysis revealed that the deterrent effect of the law occurred principally among assault-precipitated gun homicides as opposed to felony-related gun homicides. The latter type were too infrequent and erratic in occurrence to give reliable evidence of a deterrent effect.

Police and Bartley-Fox

Decision-Making Problems. The changes in Massachusetts' gun control laws that Bartley-Fox brought about presented two types of decisions for police officers. The first was in deciding whether the law applied to a particular situation they might encounter while on patrol. In particular, the law was ambiguous about whether it applied to situations within one's home or place of business. This question remained unsettled until 1978, when the Massachusetts Supreme Judicial Court ruled that it did not.

The second type of decision related to the exercise of a police officer's discretion. Even if an officer recognizes a violation of the law, he may still react to the situation in a way other than an arrest. In a situation involving a firearm, for example, he may simply seize the weapon and let the suspect go.

Level of Police Officer Understanding. The police officers whom we interviewed showed a great deal of confusion about whether the Bartley-Fox law applied in a person's home or place of business. Some of this confusion was common to others in the criminal justice system as well; defense attorneys and prosecutors also had questions about the law's scope.

Arrests for Illegal Gun Carrying. The number of incidents where the police in Boston arrested an individual for illegal gun carrying decreased after Bartley-Fox. There were 218 incidents in 1974, 186 in 1975, and 168 in 1976. Since the law had a deterrent effect with respect to assaults with a firearm, it is reasonable to assume that part of the decline in arrests for carrying illegal firearms is due to a deterrent effect of the law in that type of behavior as well as assaults.

Since Bartley-Fox presented the risk of a one-year jail sentence for anyone arrested for a gun-carrying charge, there was some speculation that police officers would decline to arrest individuals after the law went into effect in an effort to avoid the new, harsher sentence. We examined police behavior in the city of Boston to determine if this were so. As a measure of police reaction to Bartley-Fox, we looked at situations involving a potential carrying arrest and determined how often Boston police officers in these circumstances arrested individuals who were involved, rather than merely seizing the weapon and making no arrest. Based upon this information, we found no evidence that there was any widespread evasion of the Bartley-Fox law by Boston police officers.

Most of the incidents involving a potential arrest for gun carrying occurred outdoors. Location is an important factor because, as we have mentioned, there was an element of uncertainty concerning the law's application in some locations (the person's home or business). In the year before Bartley-Fox went into effect and in the two years afterward, when the gun-carrying incident occurred out of doors, there was no statistically significant change in the rate at which police officers would make an arrest as opposed to simply a seizure of the firearm. Thus, in situations that presented no ambiguity

about the application of the law, there was no evidence that
Boston police officers declined to make valid arrests.

When, on the other hand, ambiguity did exist, there was a
change in police arrest behavior. In 1975, the first year of
Bartley-Fox, when the incident occurred in the home of the
person who possessed the firearm, there was an *increase* in the
proportion of cases in which the police made an arrest rather
than simply a seizure of the weapon. Instead of any attempt
to avoid the Bartley-Fox law, there was a more frequent use
of arrests in situations involving a firearm in possessors'
homes. However, the trend was reversed in 1976, the law's
second year, when there was less frequent use of police officers' arrest power in incidents in the possessors' homes than
in 1974.

One possible explanation for this change in the rate of arrests is that in 1975 a great deal of public attention was focused on Bartley-Fox cases in general. In this atmosphere, the
police, presented with a situation in which the law's application was unclear, resolved the doubt in favor of vigorous enforcement. The element of public attention was absent in
1976 and so was the phenomena of an increased arrest rate.

What we see then is that in a small area of police behavior, where the application of the law was unclear, police officers responded to a one-year mandatory minimum sentence
provision by increasing their rate of arrest in the law's first
year and decreasing it in the second. While we discovered
some isolated instances which were not officially reported,
where police officers declined to make an arrest because of
the one-year mandatory sentence, we found no widespread
pattern of evasion.

No Apparent Racisim. One of the fears surrounding the
enactment of the Bartley-Fox law was that the creation of a
one-year mandatory minimum sentence would be enforced in
a discriminatory way. For example, police officers might use
the law in a different manner when they dealt with non-white
suspects than with whites. From our examination of Boston
Police Department data, we concluded that there is no evi-

dence of a racially discriminatory pattern of Bartley-Fox enforcement. In 1974, before the law was passed, the rate at which whites were arrested for gun control crimes as opposed to merely having the firearm seized was just about the same as for non-whites. After Bartley-Fox, there was still no significant difference between whites and non-whites.

Citizens' Turning in Firearms to the Police. In 1974, before the Bartley-Fox law went into effect, private citizens voluntarily turned in twenty-one firearms to the Boston Police Department. In 1975, when illegal gun carrying became subject to a one-year mandatory minimum sentence, 106 firearms were handed over, as were eighty-six in 1976. Whites increased their gun hand-in activity to a greater extent than did non-whites.

The Charging Decision

Once a police officer makes an arrest, the next decision in the criminal justice system is the charging decision. If a defendant is charged with illegally carrying a firearm, he is subject to the mandatory minimum sentence; on the other hand, if a defendant is charged with illegal possession of a firearm, he is not. The two types of conduct are similar. Carrying is simply possession plus movement. Because of this similarity and because of the discretion that charging authorities have in determining which charge to bring, it is possible that possession charges would be brought when carrying charges were otherwise appropriate. If possession charges are used in this manner, it would be one way to avoid the rigidity of the Bartley-Fox sentencing policy.

Who Makes the Charging Decision? In general, the decision to bring either a carrying charge or possession charge is made in the district court. In Boston, during the three years of our study, the major responsibility for deciding the charge was with the arresting officer, who often consulted with other police officers and court personnel. Once a police officer decided to request a particular charge, court officials rarely refused to grant it. The one exception to this pattern was in the Boston Municipal Court, where judges rather than clerk's office personnel decided which charge was appropriate.

In Springfield, judges, clerks, and prosecutors took a more active role in deciding the charge than in Boston.

Charging Officials' Understanding of the Difference Between Carrying and Possession. The police officers, who have a great deal of influence over which charge is brought, showed a considerable amount of confusion over the difference between carrying and possession. For example, 12 percent of the officers interviewed said there was no difference, while 31 percent said they did not know the difference. There was also a degree of confusion among defense attorneys and prosecutors about the difference between the two crimes.

Avoidance of the Mandatory Sentence. Did the charging authorities use a possession charge rather than a carrying charge in order to avoid the mandatory minimum sentence of the Bartley-Fox law? Charging policy varied in the different jurisdictions that we examined. In Springfield, for example, prosecutors, judges, and clerks all admitted that very often they deliberately used a possession charge as a substitute for a carrying charge. If a defendant convicted of possession deserved to go to jail, the judge could still send him, but his hands were not tied in advance.

In the Boston courts, we looked at the ratio of carrying charges to possession charges to see if Bartley-Fox had an effect on the charging authorities' decision to use possession instead of a Bartley-Fox charge. In the Boston Municipal Court where judges conducted the hearing to determine the proper charge, there was no change in the use of carrying charges after Bartley-Fox. In the other district courts in the City of Boston, there was a change.

In the other Boston courts, carrying charges were used more frequently in 1975, Bartley-Fox's first year, compared to possession charges than in 1974. In 1976, this trend reversed; the use of carrying compared to possession went down—below the 1974 level. We spoke with attorneys who represented defendants in the 1976 case sample who were charged with possession and not with carrying. We were able to identify at least five cases where a carrying charge rather than a possession charge would have been appropriate. This pattern of a vigorous use of the Bartley-Fox charge in 1975, followed by a decline in 1976, is the same as the pattern we found in the area of arrest. Both these areas are controlled by the police and may have been a factor of increased public attention in the law's first year.

No Discriminatory Pattern. As with the arrest area, during the public debate over the Bartley-Fox law there was concern that the law would fall unjustly upon minority defendants in the charging decision. Our examination of court records reveals that there was no racial discrimination pattern of charging a defendant with carrying rather than possession. If anything, white defendants are charged more with carrying and at a greater rate than non-whites. This phenomenon, however, may not be a factor of racial discrimination so much as it is of different charging policies in different parts of the city. Roxbury District Court, which is almost all non-white, had a charging pattern after Bartley-Fox that used a carrying charge far less often compared to possession than did other district courts in heavily white areas.

Disposition of Cases

The major change in the law brought about by Bartley-Fox was at the sentencing stage of a gun-carrying case. Bartley-Fox imposed a mandatory minimum sentence of one year in jail. Suspended sentences or probation were prohibited.

The Bartley-Fox law also prohibited continuing cases without a finding, or filing them, methods once used by the courts to avoid giving someone a criminal record even though he or she might be guilty.

The total number of gun-carrying cases declined after Bartley-Fox went into effect. This decline follows from our other findings that gun assaults declined, as did arrests involving only a gun-carrying offense.

Proportion of Defendants Convicted. One major effect

that Bartley-Fox had on the court system was to decrease the proportion of defendants who were convicted of illegally carrying a firearm. In 1974, almost half of all gun-carrying defendants (48.6 percent) were eventually convicted. In the two years after the law went into effect, 1975 and 1976, the rate of conviction fell to about one-fourth of all defendants (28.2 percent in 1975, 22.2 percent in 1976). The decline in convictions came about primarily at the Superior Court level.

Proportion of Gun-Carrying Defendants Who Went to Jail. Although the proportion of defendants who were convicted fell, the proportion who received some jail sentence increased. In 1974, 11.1 percent of all gun-carrying defendants received a jail sentence. The rest of the 48.6 percent who were convicted received either a suspended sentence, probation, or a fine. Once Bartley-Fox became law, all those convicted received a jail sentence. In 1975, 28.2 percent of all the defendants who faced a gun-carrying charge were sentenced to jail, as were 21.3 percent in 1976.

Thus, one effect of Bartley-Fox was to increase the proportion of defendants going to jail but at the expense of decreasing the proportion who were subject to some sanction from the court. It is fair to conclude that some people who would have received a suspended sentence prior to Bartley-Fox now receive no sanction whatsoever.

Of the defendants who received a jail sentence for gun carrying under Bartley-Fox, some would have gone to jail even if there were no mandatory minimum sentence in effect. For each of the two years of Bartley-Fox examined in the City of Boston (1975 and 1976), we tried to determine how many people received a jail sentence that would not have occurred without the mandatory minimum sentence. We could only make a rough approximation of this phenomenon.

We looked at all those sentenced to jail in 1975 and 1976. We excluded those whose jail sentence was harsher than the one-year mandatory minimum sentence. We also excluded those whose one-year sentence for gun carrying was concurrent with a longer sentence for another crime. The Bartley-Fox sentence in these cases was of no practical effect. Of the cases that were left, we can conclude that the defendants may have gone to jail only because of the mandatory minimum sentencing provision. We were conservative in making our estimate, so as not to underestimate the effect of the law. Our results were these: For the half-year sample in 1975, we found only twenty cases where Bartley-Fox *may* have been the cause of the jail sentence. In the half-year sample for 1976, we found seventeen such cases.

Extrapolating over a full year in Boston, the change in sentencing brought about by Bartley-Fox affected *at most* about forty people each year, a particularly small number when compared with the effect the law had in reducing gun-related crime.

Did Bartley-Fox Change District Courts' Handling of Gun-Carrying Cases? The district courts in Massachusetts are the entry-level courts for almost all criminal cases. They hold trials for most misdemeanors and minor felony cases, and they hold probable cause hearings for serious felony cases that can only be tried in the Superior Court.

Before Bartley-Fox went into effect, 59 percent of the time the district courts in Boston disposed of gun-carrying cases adverse to defendants by convicting them, or finding probable cause and sending the case on for trial in Superior Court. In 1975, the rate at which district courts ruled against the defendant was 55 percent, and in 1976, 54 percent. This difference was not statistically significant. Boston district courts, in the aggregate, thus either convicted or found probable cause in gun-carrying cases in just about the same proportion after Bartley-Fox as before.

There was a change, however, in the methods that the courts used to rule in favor of the defendant. Bartley-Fox prohibited continuing cases without a finding or filing them. In 1974, the district courts disposed of 9 percent of their gun-carrying cases in these ways. After Bartley-Fox, no cases were treated in this manner—rather the dismissal and not-guilty rates increased.

One other change occurred after Bartley-Fox in the Boston district courts: The defendants who were found guilty appealed their cases for a trial de novo at a far higher rate. In 1974, 20 percent of those convicted in the district courts went on for a trial de novo. In 1975, when the one-year mandatory sentence began, that figure rose to 89 percent and went to 95 percent in 1976. Thus, upping the ante for defendants by imposing a mandatory jail sentence has the effect of increasing their incentive to take advantage of all the procedural protections built into the system.

Although the Boston district courts in the aggregate showed no change with respect to the proportion of gun-carrying cases in which they ruled against the defendant, individual courts did change. Before Bartley-Fox, some courts were prosecution-prone and others defendant-prone. After Bartley-Fox, they all came to meet somewhere within a relatively narrow middle range. The law thus promoted some degree of uniformity.

However, in individual courts in some cases, we believe there was a pattern of evasion of the Bartley-Fox law by disproportionately ruling in favor of the defendant in a gun-carrying case. In our 1976 case sample, we interviewed attorneys who represented Bartley-Fox defendants whose cases had been dismissed or found not guilty in the district court. We were able to identify six cases where a fair conclusion is that the judge's sympathy to the defendant or antipathy to Bartley-Fox played a role. Our general interviews with defense attorneys, prosecutors, and judges all revealed a commonly shared perception that some judges do favor defendants in Bartley-Fox cases.

Superior Court's Handling of Gun-Carrying Cases. As mentioned, after Bartley-Fox became law, a higher proportion of gun-carrying cases were disposed of at the Superior Court level than before. Bartley-Fox did bring about a change in how the Superior Court handled these cases. Of most significance is the decline in the proportion of defendants convicted. In 1974, 71 percent of the gun-carrying cases disposed of by the Superior Court were convictions. This fell to 52 percent in 1975, and 44 percent in 1976.

This decline came about in two ways. First, a smaller proportion of defendants chose to plead guilty to gun carrying after Bartley-Fox, and a higher proportion went to trial. Second, defendants who went to trial after Bartley-Fox stood a much better chance of winning the case than before. In 1974, 91 percent of the gun-carrying trials ended up with a guilty verdict. In 1975, only 44 percent did, and in 1976, only 35 percent. This decrease in the conviction rate was true for both jury trials and trials before a judge alone.

There are two possible explanations for the decrease in the conviction rate. First, more weak prosecution cases are going to trial. With only the possibility of a jail sentence, defendants were less likely to accept a district court conviction or a guilty plea in Superior Court.

The second explanation is that the jury or judge evaluated the testimony with a slant toward acquitting the defendant because of the mandatory one-year sentence. We observed a Bartley-Fox trial where the defendant made no real effort to contest the facts of the case but tried in every way short of being impermissibly explicit to get the message across to the jury that this was not the sort of person who deserved to spend one year in jail. The jury acquitted. Defense attorneys, prosecutors, and judges all felt that juries were aware of and influenced by the sentencing provision of the Bartley-Fox law.

Plea Bargaining. Just as the Bartley-Fox law did not prohibit a police officer from declining to make a gun-carrying arrest or from bringing a possession charge where carrying would otherwise have been appropriate, it did not prohibit prosecutors from plea bargaining with gun-carrying defendants. A prosecutor who does not want a defendant to be subject to the mandatory minimum one-year jail term may agree to dismiss the Bartley-Fox charge in return for a guilty plea to some other crime. The prosecutor may also reduce the carrying charge to possession in return for a guilty plea. Finally, the defendant may plead guilty to a Bartley-Fox charge in return for the prosecutor's recommendation that the Bartley-Fox jail sentence be served concurrently with a longer sentence, and thus be of no practical significance to the defendant. In all three types of plea bargains, the defendant receives some advantage in return for not going to trial on the carrying charge.

Using these three types of dispositions as a measure of plea bargaining, we saw that plea bargaining continued to play an important role in disposing of Bartley-Fox cases in Superior Court. Before the law went into effect, 31 percent of the carrying cases fit into these three categories. After Bartley-Fox, the number of cases rose to 36 percent in 1975 and was 15 percent in 1976. In the two years following Bartley-Fox, in some cases, the charges were reduced or dismissed so that the defendant could receive a suspended sentence. In other cases, the defendant received a carrying sentence that had no practical effect. The Bartley-Fox law removed discretion in one area—sentencing; but discretion remained to accomplish the same ends in another area—plea bargaining.

Defendants' Decisions to Fight Their Cases. After Bartley-Fox went into effect, gun-carrying cases became a more serious matter for defendants. Not surprisingly, the rate at which they defaulted (failed to show up in the district courts), doubled. Defendants were also more prone to appeal for a trial de novo (obtaining a second chance for acquittal, or delaying the inevitable conviction) at a much greater rate. In the Superior Court, there was a trend toward an increased use of trials; although contrary to what our interviews with defense attorneys showed, there was no evidence of a preference for jury trials.

Were Prosecutors and Judges Happy?

On the whole, the judges and prosecutors with whom we spoke did not feel that Bartley-Fox persuaded those in the criminal justice system to "get tough" with violent crime. About half of them felt that the law interfered with their ability to obtain a fair and effective sentence in an individual case. Even judges with a tough reputation noted that in some cases they would have suspended the defendant's sentence if the law allowed them to do so.

GUN LAWS AND GUN COLLECTORS[2]

If firearm ownership is commonplace in America—and surveys repeatedly indicate that it is—then the firearm collectors comprise the aristocracy amid the popular movement. These collectors are virtually a "nation unto themselves," with their own shows, at which they compete in display of their finest firearms, their own organizations, their own specialities—one may choose British military firearms 1760–1945, another may strive to obtain all calibers and chamberings of the Marlin 1893. There are also general collectors, and most specialists have a general collection "on the side," which may feature such favored pieces as the exquisitely crafted Parker shotguns (which begin at about $900), the Winchester Model 21 (the only American shotgun fitted to the individual's dimensions; the "economy" line starts at $3,500), or scarce "presentation pieces," engraved and inlaid pieces given by inventors and companies to both Eastern and Western national leaders (Samuel Colt, in the 1870s and 1880s, created quite a few of these pieces). They have their own magazine now, independent of all other firearm publications, in which it is not uncommon for a collector to take out a full page, tastefully illustrated advertisement to attract other collectors for purchase or exchange of a few unneeded pieces.

Even individuals who support strict firearm regulation might well be tempted to consider these individuals a relatively riskless segment of the population. Persons bent upon robbing a drugstore simply do not seek a Winchester 21; domestic homicides are unlikely to be settled at dawn with a cased pair of Durs Egg flintlock duelling pistols. Indeed, the federal agency which enforces the firearm laws, the Bureau of

[2] Article entitled "On Turning Citizens Into Criminals," by David T. Hardy, lawyer and consultant to the Executive Director, National Rifle Association's Legislative Action Committee. *Law & Liberty.* Vol. 4, No. 4, Winter '79. Institute for Humane Studies. Menlo Park, California.

Also in *Case & Comment.* Ja.-F. '80.

Alcohol, Tobacco and Firearms (BATF), has repeatedly claimed that criminals predominantly use cheap handguns—valued under $50, caliber .32 or less, barrel 3 inches or less. No true collector would even use one of these as a paperweight: the risk of being seen with it by other collectors would be too great.

Law Enforcement Against Collectors

It is therefore surprising to note that federal agencies enforcing firearm laws have often appeared to devote a large amount of their energies to sending such collectors to jail, and confiscating their collections. It is even more surprising to discover that the federal government itself is becoming a large-scale collector—its collection established primarily by choice items appropriated, without compensation, from these collectors.

In part, the collector's very law-abiding qualities make them perfect targets for law enforcement. The BATF has been faced with some unique bureaucratic difficulties of late. Since 1972, the skyrocketing prices of sugar, main component of "moonshine," has drastically curtailed illegal brewing. Between 1972 and 1978, the number of "stills" raided by BATF dropped from nearly 3,000 to only 381. The Bureau suddenly saw itself faced with obsolescence of its traditional area of enforcement, a rather unique experience in law enforcement (one may imagine the consternation at the Drug Enforcement Administration if the entire drug-using populace suddenly turned to meditation or alcohol). Self-preservation dictated a sudden increase in firearm enforcement. But agents seeking to push up their "body counts" of arrests and firearms seized were faced with serious problems. To invade fields where firearms are feloniously used is apt to prove quite dangerous; it also takes time, and this is unavailable when Washington makes it clear that arrests in your district must be doubled within the next year. A safe and easy target had to be located.

"Dealer" Defined

Agents therefore quickly evolved a method of entrapping collectors, through a technique which I term the "implied dealership." This depends upon a clause in the 1968 Gun Control Act which provides that "dealers" in firearms must be federally licensed, and makes it a felony to conduct business as a "dealer" in firearms without such license. Private sales of one's own property by a nondealer are not subject to federal licensing.

The statute contains no definition of "dealer." Nor do the Bureau regulations, ostensibly promulgated to clarify and enforce the statute, provide such definition. Since 1972, the Bureau has actively discouraged applications for licensing, in a political move to create an impression of reduction in "firearms traffic." Under its regulations, for example, the applicant must have business premises separate from his residence and must keep regular "business hours." Collectors who reported sales only to other collectors and hours "by appointment" soon found their licenses being revoked. Moreover, a "dealer's" premises are statutorily subject to search, without warrant or probable cause. Collectors, who asked whether licenses were needed, were usually informed that five to ten firearms sales per year did not constitute acting as a "dealer."

Actually, while the statute has no definition, federal appellate courts have defined "dealer" very broadly. They have repeatedly noted that there is no minimum number of sales necessary; that no minimum level of profit from sales of firearms is essential, and that the sole question is whether the jury believes the accused citizen to have engaged in *"any* business" of selling firearms. The Bureau has frequently obtained collections on as few as four to six sales per year, and these actions have been universally upheld.

Obtaining Evidence

The agents thus can easily lead an individual, who all the while believes he is obeying the law, into a felony indictment.

Undercover agents approach the collector at a gun show. Their routine is already choreographed and has been tested in previous cases. Different agents may make one or two purchases at this gun show, followed by a few more at the next gun show, until four to six sales are obtained. The agents offer a very high price, and purchase with little bargaining; thus the collector can easily be shown to have made a profit on their sale. As "icing on the cake," they may lead the collector into stating that he could obtain an additional firearm from a different collector for them; at this point he is acting as a broker for matter not already in his collection.

After the evidence is obtained, the collector is indicted on felony charges. The burden on him is immense. Legal defense costs usually run between $3,000 and $20,000. Conviction on the felony count means total loss of right to possess firearms within the United States. It also carries a penalty of 5 years imprisonment and a $5,000 fine.

In an effort to add to these burdens, the Bureau generally confiscates the collector's prize collection. This is done under a provision of the Act which permits confiscation of firearms "involved in or used in or intended to be used in" any violation. The confiscation puts additional financial pressure on a collector who may already be impoverished by the legal costs.

These activities have been frequently reported among collectors, but little work to compile and analyze them has been done. Recently, I have had the privilege of serving as project director to a Task Force seeking to compile a comprehensive report on Bureau activities, which report was sponsored by the Second Amendment Foundation. The objective evidence which was compiled on this particular activity proved compelling. I could not escape the conclusion that the Bureau had carefully preyed upon misinformation as to the status of the law, some of which had been given out by the Bureau's own agents, in order to entrap law-abiding citizens and confiscate substantial amounts of their private property for the Bureau's own collection!

Entrapment

First, the Bureau seeks to entrap law-abiding individuals who would not disobey the law, if it were not for the agent's activities and deception; it does not aim entrapment at individuals who would violate the law anyway and are but given an opportunity. Many of the individuals contacted, in various parts of the nation, with no opportunity to confer with each other, reported acting on advice of agents that five to ten sales per year of their own firearms did not constitute "dealing." In one especially well documented case, we obtained a government transcript of a recording of the defendant speaking to the agent.

I don't want to know anybody what does anything wrong with guns. No, I'm serious. I collect, and, to me, there's a lot of fine people collecting. Several chiefs of police, several detectives here, and otherwise . . . I don't want, I would never want to contribute to anything that might make it look bad for all of us . . . There's a few people who are making it look bad for the many.

This individual was enticed into the sale of a sufficient number of firearms, his collection was confiscated at a gun show, and, when he filed suit for their recovery eight months later, an indictment was handed down within ten days. He is today a felon on probation. Given that "the first duties of the officers of the law are to prevent, not to punish crime. It is not their duty to incite to crime . . .", the entrapment of an individual of this type, solely for the virtue of increasing a "body count" of convictions and confiscations, is hardly justifiable conduct on the part of a public agency.

Confiscation

A second reprehensible aspect of the BATF attack on collectors is the tendency to focus on large and expensive collections. Confiscations tend to center upon these collections to the exclusion of the cheap firearms which the Bureau so often claims are the roots of violence. During the course of the Second Amendment Foundation study, I utilized the Freedom of

Information Act to obtain copies of the Bureau's "Reports of
Property Subject to Judicial Forfeiture," which gave inven-
tories of seizures by collector name, value, firearms, and ultimate disposal. A few examples will suffice. In one, the Bureau
confiscated 83 firearms from a Pennsylvania collector. The
Bureau's own appraisal fixed the value at $18,020. The col-
lection was devoted primarily to antique Marlin rifles, especially the 1893 model, although some 1881 models in .40–.62
caliber and an especially rare .30–.40 "baby carbine" were
included. Only five of the 83 were handguns—and the average handgun appraisal was $116. A second major example
also came from Pennsylvania. There, 136 firearms valued at
$28,335 were taken. These included five Parker shotguns (one
valued at $1,000), a Winchester model 21 (undervalued at
$900), and a number of French and German collector shot-
guns. Private reports have also been received (from time
frames outside of the period requested under the statute) of
numerous confiscations; an Eastern collector reported a seizure of $10,000 worth of items; two years after the confisca-
tion, he has neither been charged with any offense nor has the
collection been returned. A South Carolina collector reported
seizure of over 100 firearms valued at over $15,000. He was
acquitted of charges. Two weeks after the acquittal, the Bureau served him with notice of intent to forfeit his collection,
maintaining that the criminal acquittal did not bind them in
subsequent "civil" forfeiture proceedings. (Further, three
persons, in Connecticut, Arizona, and Nebraska, reported
that their automobiles were seized on claims that they had
used the vehicles to transport firearms.)

Obtaining Collections

A third reprehensible aspect lies in the Bureau's use of its
powers to furnish its own private collection. The reports obtained through the Freedom of Information Act requests
showed that approximately one-third of the collections were
being routed back to the BATF with the purpose of acquiring
a "reference collection." The two Pennsylvania seizures

mentioned earlier alone contributed 75 firearms valued at
$18,000 to this Bureau collection. The collection is not easily
filled, obviously, especially with reference to the expensive
shotguns; the Bureau apparently needed no less than *five*
Parkers, three of the same gauge. Modern firearms are also
found useful. One report from a Texas case disclosed a seizure
of 86 firearms valued at over $20,000. The local Bureau office
chose to keep 48 of these firearms for their local arsenal (and,
presumably, for issue to the agents who confiscated them). Interest in filling this collection may explain the Bureau's tendency, reported by several collectors, to dismiss charges or
permit pleas to a misdemeanor in the event the collector
would permit them to keep the collection. These offers were
transmitted through the prosecutor's office to the defense attorney's office; in several cases, I was able to contact the defense attorney and confirm that such offers had been made.

Vindictive Intent

Finally, some of the seizures appear to display a vindic-
tive intent. In a famous Texas case, the agents seizing an expensive collection were seen to deliberately drop the firearms
to the floor before storing them. Several firearms, in "as manufactured" condition and unfired, were "test fired," greatly
reducing their collector value. Despite the dealer's acquittal,
agents refused to return the firearms. Even after judgment
was rendered in the collector's favor on a civil proceeding,
they still refused. Only after contempt proceedings were
brought against them did they return the collection, then dis-
closing that it had been stored in a damp warehouse which
had seriously rusted many of the finer pieces. A Colorado defendant reported, and his attorney confirmed, that his collection (including a Parker valued at $10,000) was thrown across
the room as each firearm was booked in, and permitted to fall
to a concrete floor. A Virginia defendant reported (and, once
again, his attorney confirmed) that his firearms were thrown
into a 50-gallon drum and wheeled to court in that manner.
They were taken out and slammed down in a pile during the

trial. When a request was made to treat them more gently, the result was only more violent treatment. In several cases in addition to the Texas one mentioned above, the Bureau refused to return firearms despite acquittal and then brought civil proceedings to confiscate the collection. Some collectors reported having to give up their collection because the criminal trial had exhausted their financial resources and the legal expense of the fight would be $2,000 or more. The collector, of course, does not recover his attorney's fees in the event he is acquitted, nor does he secure the return of the firearms. The Bureau, on the other hand, is served by attorneys paid from tax funds contributed to by the dealer.

Is this apparent focus on the law-abiding gun collector an isolated occurrence, or part of a general pattern? Since the Bureau does not itemize prosecutions by collector status, it is most difficult to tell. One might expect a rational, albeit ruthless, administrator to focus upon these individuals. As noted above, they are generally naive sorts who believe that "since I am law-abiding, I have nothing to fear from the law," are unlikely to shoot informants, are easily arrested without violence, and, in short, make a perfect target for a quick increase in arrests at minimal risk. What information we do have suggests that the Bureau has been assessing its probabilities in this manner. During Project CUE, the Bureau published breakdowns of prosecutions in certain cities. In Washington, D.C., for example, out of 1,603 investigations, only 206 dealt with felons in possession of firearms, only 58 with stolen firearms, and only 20 with use of firearms in a felony. Of Chicago's 1,980 investigations, 135 dealt with felony possession, 54 with theft, and only 9 with use in a felony. Considering that studies have repeatedly documented that approximately 25 percent of handguns used in crime are stolen, one might expect that more than 3.6 percent of the Bureau's Washington investigations, for example, would deal with firearms theft. But we must reflect that catching firearm thieves and marketers of stolen firearms may be dangerous and difficult, hardly the type of thing to undertake when large numbers of quick arrests are needed.

Conclusion

In short, it appears that the Bureau of Alcohol, Tobacco and Firearms has devoted a significant portion of its investigative and law enforcement efforts to entrapping naive collectors of firearms, of a type unlikely to be contributing to criminal firearm markets. This campaign has enabled the Bureau to boast of impressive statistics of convictions and firearms seizures, with minimal effort and personal risk. It has also permitted the seizure of significant numbers of collector items, of which substantial numbers are appropriated, without compensation, for the Bureau's own collection. The underlying practice of encouraging, rather than avoiding, crime can hardly be justified: its exploitation for Bureau property gains, or as part of a vengeance motive, is even more repugnant.

THE GUN COLLECTOR'S STORY[3]

"The Fat Man," other gun dealers and collectors called him. Grossly overweight—"380 pounds easy, maybe even more," one man recalls—he haunted gun shows in the Maryland suburbs. Almost as conspicuous as his girth was his wad of $20, $50, and $100 bills. Dealers estimated he was spending $2,000 or more at a single show.

Someone once asked him why. The Fat Man identified himself as a "horse farmer" from rural Westminster, Maryland, and said he bought pistols and rifles for resale to neighbors willing to pay $50 to $100 above the market price. Dealers found the story plausible. "Farmers in isolated areas don't know values, and they don't want to take the time to look around," says one of them. "They find it's easier to give an order to a regular and let him find it, at a profit."

[3] Article entitled "The Fat Man and the Gun Collector," by Joseph Goulden, author of the best-selling *The Superlawyers* and former Washington correspondent for the *Philadelphia Inquirer. Washingtonian Magazine.* 15:86. D. '79. Copyright © 1979 by Joseph Goulden. Reprinted by permission of Brandt & Brandt Literary Agents, Inc.

Twenty-six-year-old Richard Boulin—avid gun collector, Vietnam veteran, onetime Montgomery County policeman—was among those who trusted the Fat Man: "He carried a Maryland driver's license, and he was one of the accepted crowd—not some mental weirdo who walks up to you at a show and talks funny about guns."

Still, the Fat Man was not universally liked. He often asked dealers to bend the law, to let him have guns without the transfer forms the Federal Gun Control Act requires for certain firearms transactions. He could be a pest. He would badger dealers at shows, his wad of bills always ready to furnish extra profit if they would go along with him. He would telephone them at home in the evening, pleading for particular weapons. Many dealers shied away from him.

Three times in the autumn of 1977 Richard Boulin sold weapons to the Fat Man—six pistols and a .22-caliber rifle. Each time he gave the Fat Man a careful explanation: Even though he had a federal firearms dealer's license, the weapons involved came from his private collection, not his business stock. He had obtained each of them before taking out his federal license the previous year. As far as Boulin was concerned, he was making a private sale that did not require the federal paperwork.

Boulin was wrong. First about the Fat Man, who was not a bumpkin earning a few extra weekend dollars buying guns for his rustic friends. He was a government informant, desperately trying to avoid jail on a charge of owning an illegal machine gun. His "employer," the Treasury Department's Bureau of Alcohol, Tobacco and Firearms, charged with enforcing federal gun laws, had been chillingly blunt: Either the Fat Man helped agents "make cases" against other gun dealers, or he would go to the penitentiary. Not much of a choice. So the Fat Man let the BATF agents wire his overstuffed torso with a recording device, and he put the BATF money in his overalls pocket and made overtures to dealers and collectors at gun shows in such places as the Greenbelt Armory and the National Guard hall in Baltimore.

Boulin's second mistake was, innocent intentions notwithstanding, that he violated the law. The hoariest of dicta is that ignorance of the law is no excuse for violating it. In this instance, however, the law that the 26-year-old Boulin transgressed is legal flypaper that not even competent lawyers claim to understand. Further, its enforcing agency, BATF, has deliberately left interpretations vague as to what can and cannot be done under its terms.

Richard Boulin's story is how a federal law enforcement agency used a murky law to destroy a man—and to harass hundreds of other Americans who know more about guns than they do about the intricacies of the United States Code.

Gun control is an emotional issue that has animated American politics for years, with neither proponents nor opponents getting any measure of satisfaction. Many citizens support the idea of gun control with the same fervor their hard-drinking granddaddies had for Prohibition: When asked, they're all for keeping guns out of the hands of kooky criminals. In the meanwhile, however, they keep a shotgun in the hall closet and a loaded pistol in the nightstand, and damned be any politician who tries to make off with either. The gun lobby is well financed and organized; the National Rifle Association can kick the electoral stuffing out of unfriendly congressmen, a fact well known to all politicians. Further, given the estimated 100 million to 200 million firearms already loose in America, discerning solons recognize that any prohibitive legislation short of confiscating firearms would be about as effective as a law banning procreation among English sparrows.

Nonetheless, the assassinations of the 1960s did give impetus to the notion that walking-around nuts should not be able to buy a gun as casually as they do cigarettes, and so Congress bestirred itself to pass the Gun Control Act, the federal government's first serious foray into firearms regulation.

The act required anyone "in the business" of selling firearms to acquire a federal license. It banned most interstate sales of firearms between any persons but two licensed dealers; no longer could a Lee Harvey Oswald buy a mail-order rifle through a post-office box. It required all dealer sales to be recorded on a Treasury Department form, the 44-73. It forbade sales to convicted felons, mental incompetents, drug users, and residents of a state other than the seller's.

The act contained a couple of features that critics thought Draconian. Most federal criminal laws provide for prosecution as either felonies or misdemeanors. Not so the Gun Control Act: Any violation is a felony. Nor does the prosecution have to prove criminal intent; even an unwitting technical violation is enough to land a citizen in court.

The National Rifle Association, realizing it was licked in this particular battle, tried to clear up what it considered to be deliberately fuzzy language in the statute. For instance, the act prohibits "engaging in the business without a license." The NRA's executive director, Neal Knox, aware of the brisk trading between collectors with no commercial motivation, wanted a precise definition of what constitutes a "dealer." Recalls Knox, "I had nothing but trouble, nothing but opposition, from Treasury. They said they need vague wording in order to enforce the law, to have maximum discretion.

"As so often happens when an agency is given discretion, it uses that discretion with indiscretion."

Passage of the Gun Control Act came at an opportune time for the Bureau of Alcohol, Tobacco and Firearms, which was about to go out of business as a result of the demise of the moonshine industry. BATF had begun in 1920 as the Prohibition-enforcement arm of the Treasury Department, and over the years—as it shuttled from Treasury to Justice to Internal Revenue, before emerging in 1972 as a full-blown Treasury bureau—its responsibility expanded to include tobacco and then guns. Nonetheless, for most of this time BATF was what Pappy Yokum and other up-the-hollow folks knew as "them infernal revenooer fellers."

Unfortunately for BATF's bureaucratic health, the precipitate rise in sugar prices in the early 1970s did more to wipe out moonshining than any enforcement technique ever devised by a revenue agent. BATF knocked off 2,981 stills in 1972; in 1976, agents had to scratch all over the South to find 609; in 1978, the toll dropped to 361. Clearly BATF had to find other work for its idle hands, and tobacco was not the answer, for the cigarette industry is compact and easily regulated. BATF does spar with smugglers who bring low-tax cigarettes from the Carolinas to northern cities; this campaign has produced a new American word, "buttleggers," but few results. The Mafia is now said to sell one of every five packs of cigarettes smoked in New York City.

BATF found bureaucratic salvation in the Gun Control Act. By the hundreds, it shifted agents from the moonshine beat to guns. But the bureau had a peculiar view of its mission under the law, as a former director, Rex Davis, once revealed in congressional testimony. Davis noted that about 140,000 persons held gun dealer licenses. The bureau wanted to cut down the number to around 40,000 for easier policing. As one disgruntled official of the NRA states, "BATF's enforcement priority is parallel to the way J. Edgar Hoover used to run the FBI. Agents chased teenaged car thieves rather than the Mafia, because they are easier to catch and convict. BATF goes after dealers for picayune technical violations rather than the IRA or domestic terrorist groups. Why? Easy. BATF runs up statistics that look good on paper but don't really reflect any real work."

Gun collectors, for example, are patsies for a clever BATF agent or informant, for reasons inherent in the psyche of any actively acquisitive person. Says Neal Knox of the NRA: "The problem is that some people collect guns in the same way other people collect Ming vases, but Ming vases don't come under federal law. When the guy who is a collector goes out, he may be collecting a particular kind of fine firearm, or he may be collecting a hodgepodge of guns, because his goal is to outwit his fellow collectors.

"He will try to go in like a guy swapping a pocketknife and winding up with a racehorse. He will go in with a bolt-action .22 rifle and hope to come out with a $5,000 Purdy shotgun. It doesn't happen very often, but he has a lot of fun trying."

Richard Boulin certainly had fun—until the Fat Man materialized. Boulin's love of guns began when he was a teenager; he read books on them, and subscribed to firearms magazines. During military service, he says, he was the best shot in a 300-man military police unit. After discharge in 1972, he joined the Montgomery County police department.

All the while he collected guns—not just any guns, but the fancy commemorative weapons that manufacturers produce in limited editions, fancily engraved rifles honoring Buffalo Bill or the Texas Rangers or some other historical event or figure. As a sub-specialty, he sought specific serial numbers. He was especially proud of a Golden Spike Winchester commemorative rifle numbered 20,000, last of the production run.

Over the years Boulin accumulated more than five dozen of the commemoratives. "These represented my savings," he says. "My wife and I never bought stocks or stuff like that. Firearms appreciate in value just like antiques. I had thousands of bucks on my walls and in my display cases."

Boulin kept the commemoratives in mint condition. None had ever been fired—a single round through the barrel can cut the value of a collection gun by half. He wore gloves when he handled them, and even then would not touch any metal parts. His neighbors in Gaithersburg knew he collected guns, but he did not show them off.

Boulin did well as a police officer. He volunteers that his record bore two minor blemishes: for wrecking a squad car, and for napping on duty. But he had ambitions beyond a policeman's salary. So in early 1976 he obtained a federal firearms dealer's license, intending to open a part-time gunsmith shop in Damascus.

Initially, business was brisk and profitable. Many of his sales were to fellow Montgomery County policemen, secret-service agents, even an FBI man or two. "I dealt with quality stuff and quality people. The pistols I sold went for $150, $200 each. I wasn't selling Saturday-night specials to common criminals off the street."

But Boulin's dissatisfaction with police work mounted. It climaxed in mid-1976, when two officers working his shift were shot to death in a shopping center. He decided to leave the force and work for his father, an air-conditioning contractor. He also decided to get out of the gun business: The BATF paperwork was onerous, and he wanted to put full time into his new job.

And here Boulin made what even his lawyer, David H. Martin, former chief counsel for the Secret Service, admits was a mistake. As a private collector, Boulin over the years had acquired dozens of guns—pistols, rifles, and shotguns. These he did not enter into the formal bound registry book that federal law requires a dealer to maintain. He had obtained them before acquiring the license; he considered them his private collection, not his business stock.

"Unfortunately," attorney Martin says, "the way BATF applies the law, he is wrong. Once you acquire that federal piece of paper, BATF says you must put everything in the books, and put through the paperwork when you sell it."

So in selling off the remnants of his business stock, several times Boulin let go of one of his collection guns as well. He claims the mistake was an honest one, that he had the "impression that I was allowed to sell to another Maryland resident items from my private collection without going through the mandatory federal firearms paperwork."

And seven of these sales were to the "collector" that Boulin and other dealers knew as the Fat Man.

At five minutes past ten o'clock on the morning of December 14, 1977, Boulin was walking across the parking lot of his father's business in Silver Spring. He heard cars and looked up to see about ten plainclothesmen, badges on their lapels, and a host of Montgomery County policemen. He recognized one of the plainclothesmen as a BATF agent and asked if he could be of any assistance.

"Are you Richard Boulin?" one of the agents asked.

Yes. Whereupon the agents seized him, thrust him up against the side of his car, and cuffed his hands behind his back. All they would tell him was that he was under arrest for violating the firearms act.

When agents searched Boulin's car they found a loaded pistol. "We're going to charge you with carrying a concealed weapon," he quotes one agent as saying. Boulin protested that he had a Maryland license for the pistol and was permitted to carry it when he had large amounts of money with him. He pointed out that he had more than $1,000 in his wallet, money he intended to use that evening to buy a shotgun for his collection.

The agent was not impressed. "Is that personal money or business money?" one asked. Boulin bit his lip; he did not think a thief would make such a distinction. But he remained silent.

Agents thrust Boulin into the backseat of a car. "I've been an officer; I know when police are deliberately making it rough for a guy. I'm a big man; having to sit twisted in the seat, my hands behind my back, was darned uncomfortable for me, and they knew it."

During the ride to his home an agent said, "We have information you own two trained killer dogs. If they make any moves toward us, we intend to kill them."

Boulin stifled a laugh. "One of the 'killer dogs' was a miniature German shepherd, sweet as pie," he says. "She'll bark, but I don't think she even knows how to bite." The other was a nine-year-old police dog the department had planned to destroy because of a hip ailment. "I liked the dog, I didn't want to see him put to sleep, so I took him in. He was about as vicious as a sparrow."

Boulin made one request. He did not want to be paraded across his lawn handcuffed in front of neighbors. He told the agents he was a former policeman, that he did not intend to run, that he was outnumbered by about a dozen to one. Would they please remove the handcuffs?

"That's your problem," one of the agents said.

Worse was yet to come. At the house, the agents made plain they intended to confiscate Boulin's collector-weapons, which were displayed on wall racks and in cases. He protested that he had federal documentation for each of these weapons and that they had nothing to do with his firearms business. Tough luck, the agents said, and one of them appeared with a stack of canvas mail bags.

Aghast, Boulin pleaded with the agents not to put the valuable guns in such a container. A nick or scratch could de-value each gun by $50 or $100. "You're not dealing with a bunch of Saturday-night specials," Boulin said.

He got no sympathy. After more argument, the agents agreed to put the collectibles in shipping cases Boulin had stored in a barn. Boulin continued to protest the rough handling. One of the agents hushed him. "Don't worry," Boulin remembers him saying, "after the boys in the [BATF] lab in Baltimore get through with them, they won't be worth anything anyway."

By the time the agents finished, they had seized 89 firearms. "Quite an arsenal," one told Boulin. " 'Jesus,' I said to myself, 'none of these people has ever even *seen* a gun collection before.' "

The agents next drove Boulin to a federal magistrate's office in Rockville for a hearing. During the drive he complained of feeling ill, so they released his handcuffs. He says one of them dared him: "Go ahead and run; I'd like to take a shot at you."

Other BATF agents were busy elsewhere in Maryland the same hour, making further arrests—all on cases stemming from information supplied by the Fat Man. A total of 22 people were picked up. By noon, Washington and suburban radio stations were carrying BATF-supplied news of a "crackdown" on illegal gun dealers trafficking in machine guns and other weapons.

Out on bond, Boulin and his then-lawyer, former U.S. attorney George Beall, were summoned to the federal prosecutor's office in Baltimore. There he met for the first time a BATF agent named William J. McMonagle, who had been using the Fat Man as an informant for four months. McMonagle got right to the point: According to the Fat Man, Boulin had a machine gun, and BATF wanted it. Boulin quotes him as saying, "We are going to send agents out to your house to tear up the walls and the floor."

"I argued and pleaded with them for half an hour," Boulin says. "I told them that I left that sort of stuff in Vietnam, that the last machine gun I touched was in the Montgomery

County police department. I finally convinced McMonagle I told the truth."

So the agent tried another tack. The Fat Man had also told BATF that Boulin was selling guns to the Irish Revolutionary Army. "Absurd," retorts Boulin. "I made these sales [to the Fat Man] at the retail price. I would get five, six times the price if I was dumb enough to sell to the IRA—which I'm not. Hell, if I had wanted to make a buck off illegal sales, I wouldn't sell pistols for $150; I could go to New York City and sell them on the street corner for $500."

Boulin knew he was in deep trouble, so he listened to McMonagle and assistant U.S. attorney Marsha Ostrer when they offered him a deal. If he would turn informant for BATF and help make cases against other dealers, perhaps his own problems could be forgotten, or at least minimized; otherwise, he was going to jail.

"I told them I would not do the type of work they did to me—dirty work against an innocent dealer. I also told them, 'If you want me to go after machine guns and the IRA, I will help you.'" So they signed an agreement: Boulin would work as an undercover officer under the direction of McMonagle.

McMonagle's first query stunned Boulin. The agent "knew" of a ring of police officers in both Montgomery and Prince George's counties who were selling illegal machine guns. What did Boulin know about the ring? "Nothing. I never heard of it. I offered to go on the box [take a lie detector test] because I had had no approaches or contacts about any such deals."

McMonagle next showed Boulin photographs, taken with a telephoto lens, of ten persons posing with machine guns at a well-known quarry in Prince George's County. He asked Boulin to identify the men. Boulin studied the photo carefully. One of the men he had seen around gun shows, and he vaguely remembered selling him ammunition. He told this to McMonagle. "You're lucky," the agent said. "We knew you had seen him, and sold him ammunition. So you didn't lie this time."

In something of a panic as weeks went by and he could

not find anything to report, Boulin asked other gun-collector friends for leads. One man, the finance manager for a foreign car company, helped. He had heard of a person who owned an illegal machine gun. "My friend gave me this name to help me out, and I passed it to BATF. But they said, 'It's not enough. We want more.' But I refused to do dirty work for them. They finally said, 'You are noncooperative.' They canceled the agreement.

"Fine with me. Setting up innocent people goes against my fiber. I won't do it. I know what the arrest did to me. I wouldn't put an innocent guy through that wringer, not even to save my own neck."

Some days after the arrest, Boulin and his wife walked into a Rockville restaurant. He saw two police officers with whom he had worked. He stopped to say hello. One waved him away. "We don't talk to crooks. Get the hell out of here."

He went into a gun store where he had done much business. "Get out of here," the owner said. "I don't want any trouble."

Boulin heard via the grapevine that BATF was going through his record as a policeman, apparently trying to find evidence of illegal gun deals while he was with the department. A friendly lieutenant told him, "They are calling you a 'bad person.' " Boulin asked the lieutenant to testify as a character witness if he came to trial. The lieutenant sounded agreeable, but he called a few days later with an apology: A superior had ordered him to keep out of the case.

Not everyone turned his back on the former cop, however. A onetime colleague, knowing of his plight and of how law enforcement agencies work, telephoned him with a tip. He had the license number of a van being used as a rolling gun/cocaine distributorship. Give BATF the tip, the officer said; maybe the credit will help you. Boulin telephoned McMonagle. I won't talk to you about anything, the agent said and hung up.

But Boulin's main support, financial and psychic, came from the National Rifle Association. His case arose just as the NRA was gearing up a campaign against BATF's enforcement procedures. NRA's membership includes dealers and collectors targeted by BATF, and NRA is not the sort of organization that turns the other cheek.

One thing NRA did was to hire as a consultant Mike Acree, who spent almost four decades in federal law enforcement, mostly with Treasury; he retired as United States commissioner of customs. Acree reviewed scores of gun cases brought by BATF in Maryland and Virginia. He states: "I would say that, conservatively, 75 to 80 percent of those cases were individuals that, in my judgment, would not have fallen into the hands of the law had they not been enticed, inveigled, encouraged to violate some provision of law with which they were totally unfamiliar." Most of these persons—blue-collar workers, truck drivers, farmers—"simply were not sophisticated enough to understand the technicalities of the Gun Control Act." Acree accused BATF of running a "statistical rat-race kind of operation" and using questionable investigative tactics in which agents effectively persuade dealers to break the law.

One such tactic is the "straw-man purchase." As noted, a licensed dealer may sell only to residents of his own state. BATF sends an agent with out-of-state identification into a store to make a purchase. If the dealer refuses to sell to him, the agent then asks if he can have a local friend buy the gun for him and sign the transfer papers. If the dealer agrees, and makes the sale—click, out come the handcuffs.

A striking "straw man" case that got to court recently required the work of three BATF agents and an undercover officer off and on for the course of a month. The team used electronic surveillance devices—which produced unintelligible recordings—and considerable persuasion to entice Harrison W. Phillips, a Tidewater, Virginia, dealer, into a technical violation of the law. But a federal judge, after listening to BATF's case, threw the bureau out of court.

During a supposedly "routine" investigation of Tidewater-area dealers, BATF had targeted Phillips, who runs a place called Jaxon's in Parksley, Virginia. An out-of-state buyer is essential to straw-man cases, so BATF imported agent William J. Burgess from its office in Wilmington, Delaware. Two local agents fitted Burgess with a body transmitter and body recorder and sent him into Phillips's store with $200 and orders to buy a pistol.

No luck the first day: Phillips wasn't there, and BATF obviously did not wish to bother making a case on a mere clerk. So BATF sent Burgess back the next day. Patricia Burgess (no relation), a Norfolk city police officer working undercover, went along to pose as the BATF man's girlfriend. This time agent Burgess talked with a clerk and offered to buy two pistols. But when he produced his Delaware driver's license the clerk said, "Whoops!" and told him: "We can't sell to you." Another clerk asked if Burgess had any relatives "from around here" who could do the paperwork for him. Burgess mentioned the "Norfolk girlfriend" and said he would return the next day.

On the third trip the BATF team finally managed to buy a pistol. Burgess wanted two; Phillips (rightly) told him the legal limit was one handgun per working week and refused. He also (rightly) refused to let Burgess buy the .25 automatic pistol with his out-of-state license. But because his "girlfriend" stood alongside him at the counter, she was able to make the purchase, filling in the form with her name, Social Security number, and Norfolk address. Phillips wouldn't even take the money from Burgess. He insisted that the woman hand it to him, and in turn he handed her the pistol.

A week later Burgess returned and asked again if he could buy two pistols. Again Phillips refused. And, again, he insisted that Patricia Burgess handle the mechanics of the purchase. She's sitting outside in the car, ill; can't I take the forms out to her and let her sign them there? agent Burgess asked. No, replied Phillips, she must come in here. She did, and bought another pistol, a .32 revolver.

Still later in the month, Burgess obtained a Virginia driver's license—using as an address the post office of a fellow agent who lived in Norfolk—and returned to Phillips's store. He tried to buy more firearms, and showed Phillips the new license.

Phillips replied, "I know you're from Delaware. I can't sell you a firearm." He warned Burgess: "You might get sent to jail for what you are doing." Burgess left, empty-handed.

On October 4, 1977, two months after their investigation ended, BATF agents raided Phillips's shop and charged him on felony counts of selling firearms to a nonresident. They seized his entire stock—"Brownings and good guns," fifty to sixty of them—and stacked them in the trunk of a car.

Phillips's trial took less than a day, in federal court in Norfolk. Judge Dick Kellam, generally regarded as a law-and-order jurist, found his incredulity mounting as testimony proceeded. When the prosecution finished he asked, in astonishment, "That constitutes the evidence?" Yes, replied the assistant U.S. attorney, Raymond A. Jackson.

"Tell me where there is any violation of the statute in all that went on here," pressed Kellam. Jackson had nothing further to say.

"All right, gentlemen," Kellam said. "I'm going to direct a verdict. Bring the jury in."

"You're going to do what, Your Honor?" asked Jackson.

"I'm going to direct the verdict, find the defendant not guilty."

But Phillips's troubles did not end here. He had to get another court order for the return of the seized firearms—many came back rusty and scratched—and then return for another order for the restoration of his dealer's license. "It was very costly," he says of the process. "It cost me over $7,000."

In Senate testimony last summer, Richard J. Davis, the assistant Treasury secretary for enforcement and operations, tried to slough off BATF critics, and especially persons who claimed victimization at federal hands. "I think it is important to remember," intoned Davis, "that criminal investigations and enforcement are by nature conflict-oriented. Inevitably, any criminal investigation situation is bound to produce negative reaction from the subjects of investigations." Both Davis and BATF director G. R. Dickerson denied any systematic abuse of the agency's authority.

"Negative reaction" certainly describes the feelings of

David A. Moorhead, wounded eight times during the Tet offensive in Vietnam. Moorhead, a tough New Hampshire na-
tive, was listed on Army records as a paraplegic. "But I told a
full colonel I would be damned if I would stay in a wheel-
chair, and I walk today."

Moorhead returned to his home in Wentworth, New
Hampshire, and at the urging of Veterans Administration
counselors took a gunsmith course. "New Hampshire is a very
big hunting and fishing area," he says, "and there are very few
gunsmiths. It was a job I could do in my home, so I could lie
down and rest when I needed to." Moorhead opened his shop,
and began collecting firearms as well as selling and repairing
them.

BATF inspectors tested him. One undercover agent—"we
call them a snitch"—came in and tried to buy a pistol without
doing the required federal paperwork. Moorhead double-
talked him; when the man left, Moorhead reported him to the
local BATF office.

Meanwhile, through what Moorhead calls "some good old
Yankee trading," he acquired an Army surplus M-14 rifle, the
weapon he had used in the military. The training and maintenance literature that Moorhead saw referred to the M-14 as a
rifle. He made no secret of his ownership. He kept it in a display case, and state and local police were among the persons
who saw and admired it. He even listed the M-14 among his
collateral for a bank loan.

A BATF undercover man saw the M-14 in November of
1975 and talked about it with Ken Drickser, the agent as-
signed to Wentworth. Drickser is said to have told his colleagues, "If there is one [a machine gun] in Moorhead Sports
Shop, it is because he doesn't know it is one. Leave it alone
and I will take care of it when I get back from vacation."
Drickser left town on his trip.

A few mornings later, Moorhead heard someone banging
on the door of his shop. He unlocked the door, and in
swooped a raiding party of BATF agents from Boston. They
told him he was under arrest for "secretly possessing a machine gun."

Moorhead was puzzled: "It kind of confused me. I never knew I had a machine gun, and any guns I had I never knew I secretly possessed." When he realized what they wanted, he surrendered the M-14.

The agents commenced a search. They found a 37-millimeter flare gun, which is exempt from registration by BATF's own regulations. Moorhead recounts what happened next:

"I said, 'Why are you taking that?'

"He said, 'Well, we are not sure.'

"I said, 'What do you mean you are not sure?'

"He said, "Well, there are so many laws we can't be expected to know them all.'

"I said, 'You expect me to know them all?'

"He told me ignorance of the law is no excuse."

The BATF agents put Moorhead in handcuffs and took him to Concord. His wife wanted to go along "because I was subject to having muscle seizures." They refused but did permit him to take Valium. When she insisted on accompanying her husband, an agent told her she would be subject to a $5,000 fine or five years' imprisonment if she disregarded orders.

BATF agents seized thirteen other persons in four states in the same series of "raids," and the agent in charge of the Boston region said they were "significantly the largest in New England affecting licensed dealers since passage of the Gun Control Act of 1968." The headlines stood two inches tall throughout New England the next morning. The BATF release noted that "more than 100 unrecorded guns" in addition to the "machine gun" were seized from Moorhead's shop.

These, says Moorhead, were "weapons I was keeping in safe storage for local camp owners who didn't want to leave them unguarded in vacant cabins over the winter." He and his wife had listed them in a registry, which they couldn't immediately find during the confusion of the raid.

The BATF publicity was not accidental. The bureau's *Public Affairs Guidelines* manual says good public relations "is a method of overcoming the criminal defense for lack of knowledge of the law, and has a favorable impact on the attitudes of the court, jurors, and prosecutors. . . . And most important of all, it serves to establish and enhance the image and identity of the bureau with all levels of our society."

When Moorhead went on trial the following April, District Judge Hugh H. Bownes listened to testimony, then said, "I think this is a travesty. I am upset. I am really upset." He told the jury:

"I am going to do something that I haven't done since I have been a federal judge, or a state judge, for that matter. I am going to take a case away from the jury after the evidence is all closed. I don't do this because I don't have any confidence in you, but I do it because I think the circumstances require it and the law requires it."

He saw no evidence that the M-14 was a machine gun as defined by law, or that Moorhead knew it possibly could be converted. He said the BATF officers "should have used some common sense and a little compassion." Then he turned to Moorhead:

"I want to say to you, Mr. Moorhead, that, on behalf of the government, I apologize. I don't think this case should have been brought. At most, we have here a technical violation." He told Moorhead to go home.

But no gun shop awaited Moorhead's return. BATF had seized all his business records and stocks. He had to visit the VA hospital frequently for nerve pills "because I just couldn't function; I was just totally—it was just a total daze." He couldn't pay his bills; creditors demanded money. "I finally had my business auctioned off to pay my debts, which didn't clear up everything. I have since cleared up my debts by selling my home and getting this taken care of."

BATF said not a word of apology for the misdirected raid. The agency did return the seized weapons—after the intervention of Moorhead's congressman, James Cleveland.

Federal Judge Herbert Murray, who heard Richard Boulin's case, didn't exactly apologize to him. But he did indicate strongly that he felt the federal government had made a mistake in bringing the young ex-cop into court.

Months after his arrest, Boulin sought support from the

National Rifle Association, and received it in the form of
David H. Martin, a former Secret Service lawyer now with
the firm of Santarelli & Gimer. With the facts not in dispute—BATF had surreptitious tape recordings of Boulin
talking with the Fat Man during the sales—Martin decided to
try it on a question of law: Did the Gun Control Act make it
illegal for a person with a dealer's license to sell from his private collection without doing the federal paperwork? Martin
and the U.S. attorney's office in Baltimore submitted stipu-
lated facts during the summer of 1978 to Judge Murray.

Eleven months dragged by without decision, an indication
that the case was troubling Murray, a hard-working jurist. His
opinion, released August 6 . . . [1979], explained why. Under
the law, he said, he had "no choice" but to find Boulin guilty.
He continued: "The court does this with great reluctance because the potential civil penalties in this case far outweigh
the criminality of [the] defendant's conduct."

Murray referred to Boulin's prized gun collection, which
BATF still held, with the ultimate intention of having a court
declare it forfeit to the government after his conviction.
BATF has sought this, with varying success, in countless other
cases around the country. Boulin values the seized guns at between $30,000 and $35,000—provided they have not been
ruined by haphazard storage and handling by BATF. Murray
continued:

> If there were any way that this court could enjoin imposition of
> those [civil forfeiture] penalties it would do so, for the court be-
> lieves that the necessary deterrence can be achieved through the
> criminal penalties available. Further, the court has found Mr.
> Boulin to be an uncommonly cooperative defendant whose in-
> volvement in this case has been an isolated act of wrongdoing in an
> otherwise lawful and productive career.

He urged that the government work out some arrangement
whereby the guns could be sold and the proceeds given to
Boulin. And he told Martin to bring his client in later for sentencing on the eleven felony counts.

Over beer and hamburgers in a Maryland roadhouse,

Boulin talks about his life since the arrest. He is estranged from his father, who was angered by federal agents appearing at his business. He works twelve hours a day, six days a week, piling up savings to support his wife in case he has to go to prison. He drives seventy miles round-trip daily to his present job, which is in sales; all he thinks about on the road is "the case."

He is cutting himself off from a society he believes has wronged him. He talks with his wife about buying a house in rural Maryland—there are some mighty remote areas in the state—"and putting a chain across the driveway and telling everybody to stay the hell out." Most of his old police friends shun him as a "rogue cop." Neighbors avoid him, or speak in strained tones when they encounter him. Sometimes he can't bear to tell his wife about adverse developments. For months she was not aware that he would have to stand trial.

Fantasies, scenarios, awesome schemes for revenge have tumbled through his tormented head: to put his hands on a gun, a big, mean automatic gun, and go to the BATF offices in Baltimore and blast away his tormentors; to use a gun on himself; to disappear, to take what money he has saved against a jail term and simply not be Richard Boulin anymore. "But I'm past that now," he says. "There's no sense in compounding your troubles. What hasn't soaked in yet is that I am a convicted felon. A *felon*. How I'm going to live with that is something I've yet to face."

There are practical penalties to go along with the stigma. Boulin is a bonded employee. When the bond comes up for renewal, he can either admit his conviction—whereupon he loses the bond essential to his work—or he conceals it—whereupon he risks another felony charge for making a false statement. He cannot renew his Maryland state sales license, meaning he can't even sell used cars, much less have a managerial position in a first-line agency. Technically, the mortgage company could demand the full amount owed on his home. "This really worries me. BATF plays dirty; I wouldn't be surprised at all if some agent who has it in for me dropped a dime on me"—that is, notified the mortgage company of his conviction. And, of course, he cannot work as a law enforcement officer.

At age 28, thanks to his government, Richard Boulin is as close to being dead in the water as a man can be.

The Fat Man, meanwhile, is nowhere to be found on the Maryland gun scene. He has disappeared into the folds of the federal government's program to protect informants.

A postscript: Several weeks ago an openly sympathetic Judge Murray praised Boulin's record as soldier and policeman, and said he believed Boulin's protestations that he had not intentionally violated the law.

"On the other hand," the judge continued—and Boulin, standing at a military parade rest, seemed to sag—Congress passed the Gun Control Act with the aim of regulating the circulation of handguns. So Boulin must be punished. Thirty days in jail under a work-release program, so he could continue at his auto agency job, then a period of probation, plus a $500 fine.

Murray repeated what he said in his earlier opinion: that the government should work out an arrangement whereby Boulin got proceeds from the sale of the valuable firearms collection.

Three weeks later BATF still had this suggestion "under advisement," according to lawyer David Martin. Meanwhile, Martin prepared to take the case to the Fifth Circuit Court of Appeals. So Boulin has a year, maybe eighteen months, of freedom left.

I asked Boulin if he had a picture of the gun collection *The Washingtonian* could use to illustrate this article.

He laughed. "BATF took all the pictures," he said. "They called them 'contraband.' I've asked for them back, now that the trial is over, and they just laugh at me."

A VICTIMLESS CRIMES ANALYSIS[4]

Numerous commentators have warned that the criminal sanction is one that should be used sparingly. In spite of these warnings and the disconcerting experiences of Prohibition and current efforts to enforce laws against marijuana, the general response of Congress and state legislatures has been, at least until recently, to create more, not fewer, criminal offenses. The basic insight to be gained from these observers and experiences is that using criminal law to deal with social problems inevitably results in the exaction of certain social, economic and political costs, including the unintentional generation of additional crime.

In an effort to find workable legal solutions to problems and minimize such costs, legislators should rely on research results. However, one member of Congress described the federal Gun Control Act of 1968 as "political grandstanding" and a piece of "hastily drafted legislation passed at a moment of heated passion" in response to the problem of political assassinations. One policy analyst concluded that "no policy research worthy of the name has been done on the issue of gun control. The few attempts at serious work are of marginal competence at best, and tainted by obvious bias." [See Bruce-Briggs. *The Great American Gun War*.] Zimring ["Firearms and Federal Law." *J. Legal Studies*.] concludes that because of a lack of information, Congress is unprepared to make intelligent policy choices about gun control and that most members of Congress who introduce firearms bills fail to use or obtain available information.

Intelligent policymaking requires that the negative effects of gun control be weighed against the potential benefits. An analysis of the possible costs or negative consequences of a

[4] Article entitled "Enforcement Problems of Gun Control: A Victimless Crimes Analysis," by Raymond G. Kessler, instructor in sociology at Arkansas State University. *Criminal Law Bulletin*, 16:131+. Mr.-Ap. '80. Copyright 1980 by Warren, Gorham & Lamont, Inc., 210 South Street, Boston 02111. Reprinted by permission.

policy "is not, in itself, an assertion that the policy is wrong. . . . The costs comprise only one side of the equation; they may be the consequences of laws that are proper as well as those that are unwise." Unfortunately, the potentially *negative* aspects of gun control have been relatively ignored by scholars and researchers in criminology, law, and criminal justice. To aid in the formulation of policy, scholars and researchers should examine the potentially negative consequences of gun control. This discussion utilizes only one perspective from which these effects can be delineated, and its purpose is to raise issues and focus briefly on them. Resolution of these issues will require careful research.

Gun Control and Victimless Crime

The issue of whether gun control legislation has or will have a significant impact on violent crime has been much debated, and a perusal of the research reports and reviews thereof indicates that the results are mixed. Further, the methodology and conclusions of many of these studies have been questioned. The issue of the effectiveness of gun control is not resolved herein, but in view of the various methodological problems and the lack of unanimity among researchers, we must consider gun control a type of "social experiment."

A Victimless Crimes Perspective. Prohibition can be viewed as a "social experiment" which failed, and criticisms of using criminal sanctions to deal with social problems are most frequently voiced with regard to that nationwide ban on liquor and other "victimless crimes." The critics argue that such laws and their enforcement have numerous negative or dysfunctional effects. It thus appears that insight into the possible negative effects of gun control may be gained by examining the applicability of criticisms of "victimless" crime laws to gun control laws.

Defining "Victimless Crime." Probably the best-known definition of "victimless crime," by Edwin M. Schur [*Crimes Without Victims*] is: a "willing exchange, among adults, of strongly demanded but legally proscribed goods or services."

Schur discusses homosexuality, abortion, and narcotics as examples. Other crimes falling within this definition include the sale of pornography and illicit drugs and liquor, illegal gambling, prostitution, and virtually all proscribed sexual behavior involving willing participants.

The terms "victim" or "victimless" imply that someone has been harmed or victimized. But this is a conclusion based on a value judgment. Similarly, policy decisions as to whether the gains justify the negative effects of a program are ultimately based on value judgments which cannot be scientifically proven. However, the empirical consequences of policies (i.e., the extent and nature of gains and dysfunctional effects) are amenable to research, and a definition which focuses on such consequences is more appropriate for this analysis. Thus, as the discussion below will make clear, the crucial factor in Schur's approach is not the lack of a "victim" but the lack of a complainant—a person who will report the crime to the police. For this type of analysis it is more appropriate, as Schur suggests, to refer to such crimes as "complainantless." However, consensual transactions are not the only type of complainantless crime. This term also describes crimes of possession which precede and follow the illegal consensual transactions discussed above. Like such transactions, possession of relatively small items can be easily concealed from police and public, and most if not all jurisdictions have prohibited both the transfer and possession of illicit goods.

In summary, victimless or complainantless crime laws are laws prohibiting consensual transactions or possession. Thus viewed, and as will become clearer below, gun control crimes are victimless/complainantless crimes.

Liquor, Narcotics, and Gun Control Offenses. Gun control laws deal primarily with goods rather than services and are thus more similar to liquor and narcotics offenses than to other victimless crimes. The National Prohibition Act, popularly known as the Volstead Act (which ushered in the era of Prohibition) provided, with minor exceptions, criminal penalties for possessing, manufacturing, selling, bartering, importing, delivering, or furnishing intoxicating liquor. Federal and most state drug laws prohibit transfer or delivery as well as possession of narcotics.

Similarly, Title I of the Federal Gun Control Act of 1968 provides criminal penalties for certain persons who engage in certain types of firearm transactions. For example, Section 922 generally prohibits unlicensed persons from dealing in any type of firearm or ammunition and prohibits licensed dealers from selling any type of firearm to a person whom the dealer knows is under indictment for certain crimes or is an unlawful user of marijuana. Title VII of the Gun Control Act of 1968 prohibits convicted felons, persons with dishonorable discharges from the armed forces, and others from possessing any firearms in interstate commerce.

State and local gun control laws are extremely diverse. In general, they involve prohibitions against owning or carrying firearms by certain categories of persons and screening of purchase or possession through licenses, applications or permits. In general, these laws are more restrictive with regard to handguns than with ordinary rifles and shotguns. Among those prohibited from possessing handguns under various statutes are "minors, felons, aliens, fugitives, persons of unsound mind, narcotics violators and drunkards."

Recent Gun Control Bills Would Create Further Victimless Crimes. Every recent session of Congress has seen the introduction or reintroduction of numerous gun control bills that place further restrictions on handguns, ordinary rifles and shotguns. Some of the concepts reflected in these bills are (in varying combinations): national registration of handguns or of all firearms, national licensing, waiting period or police clearance as a prerequisite to handgun ownership, and prohibitions against the sale of, manufacture, transfer, importation, or possession of "Saturday night special" handguns or all handguns.

More specifically, the registration bills generally provide for maximum terms of imprisonment varying between two and five years and fines ranging between $2,000 and $5,000 for persons knowingly possessing an unregistered firearm. The handgun prohibition bills generally provide exceptions for members of the armed forces and law enforcement agencies as well as for strictly regulated and licensed importers, manufacturers, dealers, and pistol clubs. Private individuals already owning handguns would be required to turn them in and would receive reimbursement for the fair market value of the gun or $25, whichever is more. In general, violations would be punishable by imprisonment up to five years and/or a fine not exceeding $5,000. These bills would create new victimless gun control crimes; some of the possible negative consequences of these bills are discussed below.

Potential Negative Consequences

Most criticisms of victimless crime laws, their enforcement, and related matters fall into eight categories: law enforcement excesses, discriminatory enforcement and police corruption, criminal profits, bureaucratic abuse, overloading courts and corrections, labeling and corrupting effects, diversion of resources, and loss of respect for law.

Law Enforcement Excesses. The lack of a complainant and low public visibility of victimless crimes makes enforcement of the law difficult, and many government personnel resort to excesses in attempting to enforce such laws. Entrapment, unconstitutional searches and seizures, and other tactics that threaten individual security and privacy have received much attention by commentators. For instance, in their war against drugs, federal and state law enforcement agents have invaded the homes of innocent citizens, damaged their property, and subjected them to terror and abuse. Such excesses are especially likely when agents are involved in surveillance, undercover work, use of informants, and searches and seizures—all of which are utilized in enforcing gun control laws. It is thus not surprising that Zimring concludes that some of the activities of the federal Bureau of Alcohol, Tobacco and Firearms (BATF) are best compared with federal narcotics enforcement efforts.

In fiscal years 1970 through 1977, BATF alone made over

21,000 arrests and seized over 88,000 firearms. In 1977, state and local authorities made an estimated 152,900 arrests for carrying or possessing weapons, and violations of constitutional rights are not foreign to gun control efforts. For instance, Michigan court records indicate that almost 70 percent of all firearms charges have been dismissed because the evidence was obtained through unconstitutional searches. In *United States vs. Gus Cargile Residence,* a U.S. magistrate ruled that a November 1976 search and seizure of weapons was based on a warrant issued without probable cause. *Caplan vs. Bureau of Alcohol, Tobacco and Firearms* involved a suit under the federal Freedom of Information Act to obtain a copy of BATF's manual on "raids and searches." The court stated that some of the sections withheld from Caplan described "enforcement techniques that are of dubious legality under the Fourth Amendment." With regard to legislation pending in Congress, Kates [*Civil Lib. Rev.*] fears that "even partial enforcement of a handgun prohibition would result in large numbers of snoopers and informers, 'stop and frisk' laws, 'no knock' searches and other repugnant police practices."

Columnist William Raspberry [Washington *Post*] succinctly summarized the issue as follows: "It would be nice to live in a society which is both free and gunless, but I'm not sure how you can get there from here."

Discriminatory Enforcement and Police Corruption. The lack of a complainant forces the police to search for any violations they can find. In such cases they are not looking for the perpetrator of an identified criminal incident but instead "are turned loose to find a forbidden activity going on wherever they can—or want to." [Kaplan. *Criminal Justice.*] Victimless crime laws are thus easily susceptible to discriminatory enforcement based on impermissible criteria such as race, social class, or political persuasion; adding new victimless crimes only increases the potential for abuse.

In a major city with a handgun-purchase permit requirement, the police made 25,000 illegal searches in recent years " 'on the theory that any black driving a late model car has an illegal gun'—but these searches produced only 117 firearms."

Further, black ghetto residents tend to feel that they receive inadequate police protection and have mutually hostile and abrasive relationships with police. These problems were a major cause of the urban riots of the 1960s. There is some evidence that blacks and other minority group members are more likely to need, use, and possess firearms for self-protection than are whites. Zimring suggests that handgun ownership has increased substantially among members of "subcultural groups disproportionately associated with violence." Although Zimring does not identify such groups, if it is ghetto residents to whom he is referring, the effects of discriminatory or nondiscriminatory enforcement of stricter gun control laws could be disastrous. If ghetto residents are armed and ready to defend themselves against crime because they cannot depend upon the police, enforcement of strict gun control laws by the same police with whom they share a strong mutual animosity will only exacerbate police-minority hostility.

A further consequence of the lack of a complainant and the resultant potential for selective enforcement is that some law enforcement personnel can be induced to ignore violations because of monetary or other considerations violators may offer. This is especially likely to occur when the illegal activities are profitable. It is thus not surprising that the crimes most closely related to police corruption are victimless crimes such as "prohibition, gambling, drug violations, and prostitution." Violations of gun control laws can be profitable and the possibility that existing and/or proposed gun control programs may generate police corruption should be examined.

Criminal Profits. When any item for which there is demand is outlawed, illegitimate businesses will usually appear to take advantage of the profits. The legal prohibitions against gambling, liquor, narcotics, prostitution, and other "vices" have resulted in immense profits for organized crime groups, which use these profits to expand into other legitimate and illegitimate businesses, and bribe police, prosecutors, judges, and politicians.

Illegal firearms dealers have a significant impact on the

supply of "street type" firearms. One group which unlawfully transported 500 handguns into Chicago is actively distributing weapons in other large metropolitan areas as part of a larger narcotics operation. In New York City, the "black market" gun trade is a major law enforcement problem: An estimated 100,000 guns are sold each year, often at profits of 100 or 200 percent.

Zimring points out that limitations on production and imports will at some point make illicit gun production profitable and that some additional policing will be needed similar to the controls on liquor production. If limitations on handguns go into effect, the primary source of supply would be the existing civilian stockpile and the "pressure to acquire guns would drive up the price of older guns, creating incentives for both owners and prospective burglars that increase the chances that old handguns will be transferred to new owners."

Finally, since the price of goods on the illegal market will usually be higher than the price on the legal market (if one were permitted), the consumer may be forced to commit additional crimes to meet the additional cost. For instance, consider the strongarm robber who wants to obtain a handgun to increase his efficiency. He may have to commit two strongarm robberies to meet the price on the legal market, while four robberies may be necessary to afford the gun on the illegal market.

In summary, it may be that, as with other illicit goods, stricter control over firearms may mean better business for criminal profiteers.

Bureaucratic Abuse. On all levels of government, specialized squads or bureaus have been created to deal with specific types of crime, including victimless crime. The federal government, for instance, has created the Drug Enforcement Administration, which enforces laws and regulations concerning controlled substances, and the BATF, which has primary enforcement responsibilities for federal gun, tobacco, and liquor laws.

The creation of specialized law enforcement agencies may result in more efficient law enforcement, yet certain activities of such agencies raise important issues. While these issues are not necessarily confined to victimless-crime control agencies, the activities of drug control agencies have been much criticized. Packer concludes that our over-reliance on the criminal sanction to deal with narcotic and other drug violations has led to the creation of a well-entrenched bureaucracy which has a vested interest in the status quo and has thwarted major reform efforts.

Becker and Dickson trace the role of the Federal Bureau of Narcotics in the enactment and enforcement of the Marijuana Tax Act of 1937. Their analyses indicate that the Bureau became an aggressive and relatively autonomous lobbying and propaganda organization. Dickson concluded that the Marijuana Tax Act was a result of the Bureau's response to a steadily decreasing budget and its attempts to increase its scope of operations, and that as part of this campaign the Bureau diligently attacked and harassed its critics. Dickson also discusses the role of the Bureau of Narcotics in implementing the Harrison Act and suggests that through the use of its regulatory powers, the Bureau expanded its role beyond that originally intended by Congress.

It can be argued that something similar is happening with BATF. This organization has approximately 4,300 employees, a 1977 budget of $118 million and is the nation's largest gun control agency. Bruce-Briggs argues that with the decline in the illicit liquor trade the famous "revenuers" became superfluous; "BATF needs other things to do than break up stills. Since 1968 they have rapidly expanded their funding and activity in firearms control and now devote about half their personnel and budget to that function."

Proposed BATF regulations to set up a centralized firearms records system were criticized in a number of House and Senate resolutions as being an attempt to exceed the powers conferred on BATF by Congress. Both Houses of Congress then cut BATF's budget by $4.2 million, the estimated cost of the registration program, and added a prohibition against commencing the program without congressional authorization.

In summary, law enforcement bureaucracies are a threat to the democratic political process. These organizations may frequently ignore both the public interest and the long-term goals of the criminal law and often "use their resources, power and influence to obtain passage and suppression of laws that represent the interests of the bureaucracies themselves." [Chambliss. *Handbook of Criminology*.]

Overloading Courts and Corrections. While enforcement of any type of law can cause problems for courts and corrections, most commentators criticize victimless crime law-enforcement efforts for congesting and demeaning the courts and for causing pretrial delay and overcrowding of jails and correctional facilities. Many prisons are in dire need of reform, and, in numerous cases, various prison conditions have been found to constitute cruel and unusual punishment in violation of the Eighth and Fourteenth Amendments to the U.S. Constitution. Overcrowding of correctional facilities is a serious problem which may get worse. Further, the goal of rehabilitation in both traditional and community programs has generally not been realized.

Unfortunately, there is no readily available data on the number of persons currently being processed through the criminal justice system solely for victimless gun control offenses involving handguns and ordinary hunting rifles and shotguns. Such data should be gathered to assess current financial and other costs and provide a basis for projecting such costs for additional gun control laws.

In projecting these costs, one possibility that should be considered is that if new gun control laws are passed, an increasing number of defendants may be middle-class persons without prior criminal records whose offense grew out of obtaining or possessing weapons for defense of their homes or businesses. When prosecuted, it is highly likely that these defendants will demand a jury trial because of potential jury sympathy. Trial by jury is the most expensive and time-consuming method of disposition and thus the problem of crowded dockets will be exacerbated. If these defendants are acquitted, it will vitiate the deterrent effect of the law. If they are convicted, it will place further strain on correctional resources.

In sum, in the absence of massive reform and funding for courts and corrections, increased enforcement of gun control laws or the enforcement of new laws is going to result in more cases for overworked courts and more inmates for failing prisons.

Labeling and Corrupting Effects. Enforcement of laws against victimless crimes is sometimes criticized because of damage it causes to the offender's self-image and its contribution to the development of deviant subcultures. Kaplan and Becker trace these effects on marijuana users, and Schur discusses these consequences for violators of narcotics, abortion, and homosexual behavior statutes.

If the criminal market is the only available market, otherwise law-abiding citizens who want illicit goods will be forced to get them from persons in the criminal milieu who may further corrupt them. Kaplan believes this is happening with marijuana and may become a problem for otherwise law-abiding citizens who want firearms solely for the protection of their homes or businesses. While these effects may not be limited to victimless crimes, they are a factor that should be considered in the gun control controversy.

Diversion of Resources. In fiscal year 1976, total direct expenditures for criminal justice by all governments was close to $20 billion, an increase of 14.1 percent over fiscal year 1975 and of 87.1 percent over 1971. Although this is an enormous expenditure, no nation, state, or agency has unlimited resources, and expenditures for victimless crime means less expenditure for more serious crime.

In fiscal year 1977, BATF alone spent approximately $60 million on firearms control. The Bureau estimated that full administration and enforcement of the Gun Control Act of 1968 in fiscal 1976 would have required a total budget of over $331 million and a total of over 11,000 personnel.

Bills that would totally prohibit private possession of handguns and provide for compensation of persons who voluntarily turn in their handguns would be even more costly. The Justice Department estimated that the cost of compensation alone would range between $1.24 and $2.14 billion, with an additional $1 billion for administrative costs during the turn-in period. In 1975, it was estimated that the cost of national handgun registration would be $35.6 million for the first year and $21.6 million in subsequent years, and that a national handgun permit system would cost approximately $52.6 million in the first year and $21 million in subsequent years. Although some or all of these costs could be offset by registration, permit, or other fees, such a strategy only shifts the costs from taxpayers in general to handgun owners in particular. This would only stiffen their resistance to such laws. While other programs would be less expensive, it is obvious that gun control is costly. In view of the potentially negative consequences, we must ask, as did Packer with regard to gambling offenses, if these massive expenditures are justified.

Packer contends that emphasis on law enforcement solutions to the narcotics problem has stultified research on the causes, effects, and cures of drug abuse. Similarly, criminal law solutions to the problem of unlawful violence diverts resources from research and programs dealing with the social and economic forces that influence violent crime. Law enforcement solutions and the accompanying controversies, such as the seemingly endless squabbling over gun control, not only result in the diversion of resources but also in the diversion of public and congressional attention from other social issues and crime control efforts.

Loss of Respect for Law. Critics of victimless crime laws and other commentators contend that enforcement of any law that has or would have numerous and serious negative consequences and is opposed by a substantial minority or majority of citizens will result in a significant erosion of respect for the rule of law and for those who make and enforce such laws. Kates suggests that, as was the case with the prohibitions on liquor and marijuana, millions of citizens will be alienated by gun control laws which they perceive to be tyrannical. Similarly, Benenson contends that any effort to impose laws, such as stringent gun control, "which those directly effected sincerely believe oppressive and foolish inevitably leads, as with prohibition, to contempt for the entire governmental process." The overall result is thus likely to be more crime—not less. [Berrenson. *A Controlled Look at Gun Controls.*]

Conclusion

The problems generated by Prohibition helped lead to its repeal, and recognition of similar problems in drug-law enforcement has contributed to a strong movement toward reducing the penalties for, or decriminalizing possession of, marijuana. The above analysis indicates that many of the problems that have led to an outcry against crimes traditionally termed "victimless" may also result from gun control. To say that these problems will not develop because of voluntary compliance is to overlook many indications to the contrary. Critics of gun control are thus frustrated by the fact that the very segment of the community now supporting liberalization of traditional victimless crime laws is unable to recognize the similarities between those laws and gun control.

Lawmakers at all levels of government and the public in general have not given adequate consideration to the possible negative consequences of new gun control laws or to additional funding for enforcement of existing laws. The possible benefits of such laws must be balanced against the monetary and other costs outlined above. Research into the extent of such costs should be undertaken before commencing further law enforcement experiments.

Further research and analysis may help us to avoid the indictment in George Santayana's epigram that those who cannot learn from the past are condemned to repeat it.

ON THE FUTILITY OF PROHIBITING GUNS[5]

Despite almost 100 years of often bitter debate, federal
policy and that of 44 states continues to allow handguns to
any sane adult who is without felony convictions. Over the
past twenty years, as some of our most progressive citizens
have embraced the notion that handgun confiscation would
reduce violent crime, the idea of closely restricting handgun
possession to police and those with police permits has been
stereotyped as "liberal." Yet when the notion of sharply restricting pistol ownership first gained popularity, in the late
nineteenth century, it was under distinctly conservative aus-
pices.

In 1902, South Carolina banned all pistol purchases, the
first and only state ever to do so. (This was nine years before
New York began requiring what was then an easily acquired
police permit.) Tennessee had already enacted the first ban
on "Saturday Night Specials," disarming blacks and the la-
boring poor while leaving weapons for the Ku Klux Klan and
company goons. In 1906, Mississippi enacted the first mandatory registration law for all firearms. In short order, permit
requirements were enacted in North Carolina, Missouri,
Michigan, and Hawaii. In 1922, a national campaign of conservative business interests for handgun confiscation was endorsed by the (then) archconservative American Bar Association.

Liberals at that time were not necessarily opposed in
principle to a ban on handguns, but they considered such a
move irrelevant and distracting from a more important
issue—the prohibition of alcohol. To Jane Addams, William
Jennings Bryan, and Eleanor Roosevelt (herself a pistol car-
rier), liquor was the cause of violent crime. (Before dismissing

[5] Article entitled "Against Civil Disarmament; On the Futility of Prohibiting
Guns," by civil rights lawyer Don B. Kates Jr. who teaches constitutional and criminal
law and procedure at St. Louis University. *Harper's Magazine.* 257:28+. S. '78. Copyright © 1978 by Harper's Magazine. All rights reserved. Reprinted by special permission.

this out of hand, remember that homicide studies uniformly find liquor a more prevalent factor than handguns in killings.) Besides, liberals were not likely to support the argument advanced by conservatives for gun confiscation: that certain racial and immigrant groups were so congenitally criminal (and/or politically dangerous) that they could not be trusted with arms. But when liberalism finally embraced handgun confiscation, it was by applying this conservative viewpoint to the entire populace. Now it is all Americans (not just Italians, Jews, or blacks) who must be considered so innately violent and unstable that they cannot be trusted with arms. For, we are told, it is not robbers or burglars who commit most murders, but average citizens killing relatives or friends.

It is certainly true that only a little more than 30 percent of murders are committed by robbers, rapists, or burglars, while 45 percent are committed among relatives or between lovers. (The rest are a miscellany of contract killings, drug wars, and "circumstances unknown.") But it is highly misleading to conclude from this that the murderer is, in any sense, an average gun owner. For the most part, murderers are disturbed, aberrant individuals with long records of criminal violence that often include several felony convictions. In terms of endangering his fellow citizen, the irresponsible drinker is far more representative of all drinkers than is the irresponsible handgunner of all handgunners. It is not my intention here to defend the character of the average American handgun owner against, say, that of the average Swiss whose government not only allows, but requires, him to keep a machine gun at home. Rather it is to show how unrealistic it is to think that we could radically decrease homicide by radically reducing the number of civilian firearms. Study after study has shown that even if the *average* gun owner complied with a ban, the one handgun owner out of 3,000 who murders (much less the one in 500 who steals) is not going to give up his guns. Nor would taking guns away from the murderer make much difference in murder rates, since a sociopath with a long history of murderous assault is not too squeamish to kill with a butcher knife, ice pick, razor, or bottle. As for the extraordinary murderers—assassins, terrorists, hit men—proponents of gun bans themselves concede that the law cannot disarm such people any more than it can disarm professional robbers.

The repeated appearance of these facts in studies of violent crime has eroded liberal and intellectual support for banning handguns. There is a growing consensus among even the most liberal students of criminal law and criminology that handgun confiscation is just another plausible theory that doesn't work when tried. An article written in 1968 by Mark K. Benenson, longtime American chairman of Amnesty International, concludes that the arguments for gun bans are based upon selective misleading statistics, simple-minded non sequiturs, and basic misconceptions about the nature of murder as well as of other violent crimes.

A 1971 study at England's Cambridge University confounds one of the most widely believed non sequiturs: "Banning handguns must work, because England does and look at its crime rate!" (It is difficult to see how those who believe this can resist the equally simple-minded pro-gun argument that gun possession deters crime: "Everybody ought to have a machine gun in his house because the Swiss and the Israelis do, and look how low their crime rates are!")

The Cambridge report concludes that social and cultural factors (not gun control) account for Britain's low violence rates. It points out that "the use of firearms in crime was very much less" before 1920 when Britain had "no controls of any sort." Corroborating this is the comment of a former head of Scotland Yard that in the mid-1950s there were enough illegal handguns to supply any British criminal who wanted one. But, he continued, the social milieu was such that if a criminal killed anyone, particularly a policeman, his own confederates would turn him in. When this violence-dampening social milieu began to dissipate between 1960 and 1975, the British homicide rate doubled (as did the American rate), while British robbery rates accelerated even faster than those in America. As the report notes, the vaunted handgun ban proved completely ineffective against rising violence in Britain, although the government frantically intensified enforcement and extended controls to long guns as well. Thus, the Cambridge study—the only in-depth study ever done of English gun laws—recommends "abolishing or substantially reducing controls" because their administration involves an immense, unproductive expanse and diverts police resources from programs that might reduce violent crime.

The latest American study of gun controls was conducted with federal funding at the University of Wisconsin. Advanced computerized techniques allowed a comprehensive analysis of the effect of every form of state handgun restriction, including complete prohibition, on violence in America. Published in 1975, it concludes that "gun-control laws have no individual or collective effect in reducing the rate of violent crime."

Many previous studies reaching the same conclusion had been discounted by proponents of a federal ban, who argued that existing state bans cannot be effective because handguns are illegally imported from free-sale states. The Wisconsin study compared rates of handgun ownership with rates of violence in various localities, but it could find *no correlation.* If areas where handgun ownership rates are high have no higher per capita rates of homicide and other violence than areas where such rates are low, the utility of laws designed to lower the rates of handgun ownership seems dubious. Again, the problem is not the "proliferation of handguns" among the law-abiding citizenry, it is the existence of a tiny fraction of irresponsible and criminal owners whom the law cannot possibly disarm of these or other weapons.

Far from refuting the Wisconsin study, the sheer unenforceability of handgun bans is the main reason why most experts regard them as not worth thinking about. Even in Britain, a country that, before handguns were banned, had less than one percent of the per capita handgun ownership we have, the Cambridge study reports that "fifty years of very strict controls has left a vast pool of illegal weapons."

It should be emphasized that liberal defectors from gun confiscation are no more urging people to arm themselves

than are those who oppose banning pot or liquor necessarily
urging people to indulge in them. They are only saying that
national handgun confiscation would bring the federal government into a confrontation with millions of responsible citizens in order to enforce a program that would have no effect
upon violence, except the negative one of diverting resources
that otherwise might be utilized to some effective purpose.
While many criminologists have doubts about the wisdom of
citizens trying to defend themselves with handguns, the lack
of evidence to justify confiscation requires that this remain a
matter of individual choice rather than government fiat.

Nor can advocates of gun bans duck the evidence adverse
to their position by posing such questions as: Why should
people have handguns; what good do they do; why *shouldn't*
we ban them? In a free country, the burden is not upon the
people to show why they should have freedom of choice. It is
upon those who wish to restrict that freedom to show good
reason for doing so. And when the freedom is as deeply valued by as many as is handgun ownership, the evidence for infringing upon it must be very strong indeed.

If the likely benefits of handgun confiscation have been
greatly exaggerated, the financial and constitutional costs
have been largely ignored. Consider the various costs of any
attempt to enforce confiscation upon a citizenry that believes
(whether rightly or not) that they urgently need handguns for
self-defense and that the right to keep them is constitutionally
guaranteed. Most confiscationists have never gotten beyond
the idea that banning handguns will make them magically
disappear somehow. Because they loathe handguns and consider them useless, the prohibitionists assume that those who
disagree will readily turn in their guns once a national confiscation law is passed. But the leaders of the national handgun
prohibition movement have become more realistic. They recognize that defiance will, if anything, exceed the defiance of
Prohibition and marijuana laws. After all, not even those who
viewed drinking or pot smoking as a blow against tyranny
thought, as many gun owners do, that violating the law is necessary to the protection of themselves and their families.

Moreover, fear of detection is a lot more likely to keep citizens from constant purchases of liquor or pot than from a single purchase of a handgun, which, properly maintained, will last years.

To counter the expected defiance, the leaders of the national confiscation drive propose that handgun ownership be punished by a nonsuspendable mandatory year in prison. The mandatory feature is necessary, for otherwise prosecutors would not prosecute, and judges would not sentence, gun ownership with sufficient severity. The judge of a special Chicago court trying only gun violations recently explained why he generally levied only small fines: The overwhelming majority of the "criminals" who come before him are respectable, decent citizens who illegally carry guns because the police can't protect them and they have no other way of protecting themselves. He does not even impose probation because this would prevent the defendants, whose guns have been confiscated, from buying new ones, which, the judge believes, they need to live and work where they do.

These views are shared by judges and prosecutors nationwide; studies find that gun-carrying charges are among the most sympathetically dealt with of all felonies. To understand why, consider a typical case that would have come before this Chicago court if the D.A. had not dropped charges. An intruder raped a woman and threw her out of a fifteenth-floor window. Police arrived too late to arrest him, so they got her roommate for carrying the gun with which she scared him off when he attacked her.

Maybe it is not a good idea for this woman to keep a handgun for self-defense. But do we really want to send her to federal prison for doing so? And is a mandatory year in prison reasonable or just for an ordinary citizen who has done nothing more hurtful than keeping a gun to defend herself—when the minimum mandatory sentence for murder is only seven years and most murderers serve little more?

Moreover, the kind of nationwide resistance movement that a federal handgun ban would provoke could not be broken by imprisoning a few impecunious black women in Chicago. Only by severely punishing a large number of respectable citizens of every race and social class would resisters eventually be made to fear the law more than the prospect of living without handguns in a violent society. At a very conservative estimate, at least half of our present handgun owners would be expected to defy a federal ban. I reach this estimate in this fashion: Surveys uniformly find a majority of gun owners support gun registration—in theory. In practice, however, they refuse to register because they believe this will identify their guns for confiscation if and when a national handgun ban eventually passes. In 1968, Chicago police estimated that two-thirds of the city's gun owners had not complied with the new state registration law; statewide noncompliance was estimated at 75 percent. In Cleveland, police estimate that almost 90 percent of handgun owners are in violation of a 1976 registration requirement. My estimate that one out of two handgun owners would defy national confiscation is conservative indeed when between two out of three and nine out of ten of them are already defying registration laws because they believe such laws presage confiscation. To imprison just one percent of these 25 million people would require several times as many cells as the entire federal prison system now has. The combined federal, state, and local jail systems could barely manage. Of course, so massive an enforcement campaign would also require doubling expenditure for police, prosecutors, courts, and all the other sectors of criminal justice administration. The Wisconsin study closes with the pertinent query: "Are we willing to make sociological and economic investments of such a tremendous nature in a social experiment for which there is no empirical support?"

The argument against a federal handgun ban is much like the argument against marijuana bans. It is by no means clear that marijuana is the harmless substance that its proponents claim. But it would take evidence far stronger than we now have to justify the enormous financial, human, institutional, and constitutional costs of continuing to ferret out, try, and imprison even a small percentage of the otherwise law-abiding citizens who insist on having pot. Sophisticated analysis of the criminalization decision takes into account not only the harms alleged to result from public possession of things like pot or guns, but the capacity of the criminal law to reduce those harms and the costs of trying to do so. Unfortunately most of the gun-control debate never gets beyond the abstract merits of guns—a subject on which those who view them with undifferentiated loathing are no more rational than those who love them. The position of all too many gun-banning liberals is indistinguishable from Archie Bunker's views on legalizing pot and homosexuality: "I don't like it and I don't like those who do—so it ought to be illegal."

The emotionalism with which many liberals (and conservatives as well) react against the handgun reflects not its reality but its symbolism to people who are largely ignorant of that reality. A 1975 national survey found a direct correlation between support for more stringent controls and the inability to answer simple questions about present federal gun laws. In other words, the less the respondent knew about the subject, the more likely he was to support national confiscation. Liberals advocate severely punishing those who will defy confiscation only because the liberal image of a gun owner is a criminal or right-wing fanatic rather than a poor black woman in Chicago defending herself against a rapist or a murderer. Contrary to this stereotype, most "gun nuts" are peaceful hobbyists whose violence is exclusively of the Walter Mitty type. Gun owners' views are all too often expressed in right-wing terms (which does nothing for the rationality of the debate) because twenty years of liberal vilification has given them nowhere else to look for support. If only liberals knew it, handgun ownership is disproportionately high among the underprivileged for whom liberals traditionally have had most sympathy. As the most recent (1975) national demographic survey reports: "The top subgroups who own a gun *only* for self-defense include blacks (almost half own one for this reason alone), lowest income group, senior citizens." The average liberal has no understanding of why people have guns because he has no idea what it is like to live in a ghetto where police have given up on crime control. Mi-

nority and disadvantaged citizens are not about to give up
their families' protection because middle-class white liberals
living and working in high-security buildings and/or well-po-
liced suburbs tell them it's safer that way.

A final cost of national gun confiscation would be the vast
accretion of enforcement powers to the police at the expense
of individual liberty. The Police Foundation, which ardently
endorses confiscation, recently suggested that federal agencies and local police look to how drug laws are enforced as a
model of how to enforce firearms laws. Coincidentally, the
chief topic of conversation at the 1977 national conference of
supporters of federal confiscation was enforcement through
house searches of everyone whom sales records indicate may
ever have owned a handgun. In fact, indiscriminate search,
complemented by electronic surveillance and vast armies of
snoopers and informers, is how handgun restrictions are enforced in countries like Holland and Jamaica, and in states
like Missouri and Michigan. Even in England, as the Cambridge report notes, each new Firearms Act has been accom-
panied by new, unheard-of powers of search and arrest for the
police.

These, then, are the costs of banning handguns: even attempting an effective ban would involve enormous expenditures (roughly equal to the present cost of enforcing all our
other criminal laws combined) to ferret out and jail hundreds
of thousands of decent, responsible citizens who believe that
they vitally need handguns to protect their families. If this
does not terrorize the rest of the responsible handgun owners
into compliance, the effort will have to be expanded until
millions are jailed and the annual gun-banning budget closely
seconds defense spending. And all of this could be accomplished only by abandoning many restraints our Constitution
places upon police activity.

What would we have to show for all this in terms of crime
reduction? Terrorists, hit men, and other hardened criminals
who are not deterred by the penalties for murder, robbery,
rape, burglary, et cetera are not about to be terrified by the
penalties for gun ownership—nor is the more ordinary mur-

derer, the disturbed, aberrant individual who kills out of rage rather than cupidity.

What we should have learned from our experience of Prohibition, and England's with gun banning, is that violence can be radically reduced only through long-term fundamental change in the institutions and mores that produce so many violent people in our society. It is much easier to use as scapegoats a commonly vilified group (drinkers or gun owners) and convince ourselves that legislation against them is an easy short-term answer. But violence will never be contained or reduced until we give up the gimmicky programs, the scapegoating, the hypocritical hand-wringing, and frankly ask ourselves whether we are willing to make the painful, disturbing, far-reaching institutional and cultural changes that are necessary.

BIBLIOGRAPHY

An asterisk (°) preceding a reference indicates that the article or part of it has been reprinted in this book.

BOOKS AND PAMPHLETS

Alviani, J. D. and Drake, W. R. Handgun control: issues and alternatives. Handgun Control Project, U.S. Conference of Mayors, Washington, D.C. 1975.

Block, Irvin. Gun control: one way to save lives. Public Affairs Pamphlet #536. Public Affairs Committee. '76.

Davidson, Bill R. To keep and bear arms. Sycamore Island. '79.

Dolan, E. F. Gun control. Watts. '78.

Edwards, J. E. Myths about guns. Peninsula Press. '78.

Fordham Urban Law Journal. Vol. 5, No. 1. Fall '76. Restoring the balance: the second amendment revisited. David I. Caplan.

Gottlieb, Alan B. The gun owner's political action manual. Green Hill. '76.

Gun control (Legislative Analyses Series). Am Enterprise. '76.

Gun control means people control. Ind American. '74.

Hardy, David T. and John Stompoly. Of arms and the law. Second Amendment Foundation Series.
Also: Chicago-Kent Law Review. Vol. 51, No. 1. Summer '74. p 62–114.

Kates, Don B. Jr., ed. Restricting handguns; the liberal skeptics speak out. North River Press. '79.

Knox, Neil. Gun laws don't reduce crime. National Shooting Sports Foundation.

Kukla, Robert J. Gun control: a written record of efforts to eliminate the private possession of firearms in America. Stackpole. '73.

Sandys-Winsch, Godfrey. Gun laws. Shaw & Sons. '79.

Sherrill, Robert. The Saturday night special. Penguin. '75.

Whisker, James B. The citizen soldier and U.S. military policy. North River Press. '79.

William & Mary Law Review. Vol. 20, No. 2. Winter '78. p 235–90. Firearm ownership and regulation: Tackling an old problem with renewed vigor. David T. Harvey.

PERIODICALS

American Journal of Psychology. 137:121–2. Ja. '80. Influence of gun control laws on suicidal behavior. David Lester and Mary Murrell.

American Opinion. 22:5–6+. S. '79. American liberty and your right to your gun. Alan Stang.

American Opinion. 22:11–16+. O. '79. Suddenly even liberals are oposing gun control. Alan Stang.

American Rifleman. 127:N2. O. '79. Carter issues NRA statement on Gavett court case decision.

American Rifleman. 127:N7. N. '79. Representative Volkmer introduces reform bill.

American Rifleman. 128:N1. Ja. '80. Evidence of growth presented by NRA's Board of Directors.

American Rifleman. 128:N11. Ja. '80. Congressman Bauman pushes for Justice inquiry.

American Rifleman. 128:J5. Mr. '80. Latest Gallup poll confirms DMI.

American Rifleman. 128:J5. Mr. '80. Urge support of reform effort (Volkmer-McClure Act on firearms).

American Rifleman. 128:J6. Mr. '80. Anti-gun elitist? Jack Lord.

American Rifleman. 128:J6. Mr. '80. NRA members can shape party lines.

American Rifleman. 128:46. Ap.'80. Federal firearms reform act. James A. McClure.

American Rifleman. 128:98. Jl. '80. Mixed bag. Jim Rikhoff.

American Sociological Review. 45:229+. Ap. '80. Firearms ownership for sport and protection: two divergent models. Alan J. Lizotte and David J. Bordua.

°Business & Society Review. Fall '77. 67–71. Showdown with gun gang at gun control corral: our country is armed against itself. M. K. Beard.

°Changing Times. 33:33–6. Ag. '79. Noncombatant's guide to the gun control fight.

Christian Century. 96:469–71. Ap. 25 '79. Gun deaths—some real, dead cases.

°Criminal Law Bulletin. 16:131+. Ap. '80. Enforcement problems of gun control: a victimless crimes analysis. R. G. Kessler.

°Criminal Law Bulletin. 16:150+. Ap. '80. Massachusetts' mandatory minimum sentence gun law: enforcement, prosecution, and defense impact. David Rossman, Paul Froyd, G. L. Pierce, John McDevitt, W. J. Bowers.

Economic Outlook USA. 5:54+. Summer '78. The gun control

issue and public attitudes. Howard Schuman and Stanley Presser.

Esquire. 90:20. S. 26, '78. Help needed on gunrunning.

Evaluation Quarterly. 1:543038. N. '77. The effect of Massachusetts' gun control law on gun-related crimes in the city of Boston.

Field and Stream. 83:46+. Mr. '78. Handgun control: a different view. Don B. Kates Jr.

Field and Stream. 83:14+. S. '78. Rex and Richard . . . and Jimmy; Bureau of Alcohol, Tobacco and Firearms' plan to set up a computerized national registration system. E. B. Mann.

Field and Stream. 83:4. N. '78. Editor; Harris poll on attitudes toward guns. Jack Samson.

Field and Stream. 83:102–4+. F. '79. Stick to your guns. Bob Brister.

Field and Stream. 83:4 (editorial). Mr. '79. Bill of Rights: right to keep and bear arms. D. E. Petzal.

Field and Stream. 83:32–3. Ap. '79. Inventory your guns. J. J. Knap.

Field and Stream. 83:180+. Ap. '79; 84:152+. My. '79. News for '79. Bob Brister.

Field and Stream. 84:34–5+. Jl. '79. Gun control: the real facts; Excerpt from Handgun Restrictions. Don B. Kates Jr.

Field and Stream. 84:32. F. '80. Our endangered tradition. E. B. Mann.

Field and Stream. 85:16+. Je. '80. Assassination record. E. B. Mann.

Field and Stream. 85:22. Jl. '80. Gun ownership views. E. B. Mann

°Field and Stream. 85:10+. Ag. '80. Gun laws vs. crime. An exclusive interview with Senator Edward M. Kennedy, and comments by firearms-law authority. Don B. Kates Jr.

°Field and Stream. 85:16–17+. Ag. '80. Polls, good and bad. E. B. Mann.

°Gallup Opinion Index. p 28–32. Ja. '80. Public favors stricter curbs on handguns but opposes ban.

°Guns and Ammo. 23:6. My. '79. Washington report. Jim Oliver.

Guns and Ammo. 23:31. Je. '79. A disarmed citizen is a defenseless citizen. Jerry Ahern.

Guns and Ammo. 23:3. Jl. '79. Ban-the-handgun crowd: aiming at the American woman. Beverley Combs.

Guns and Ammo. 23:30. O. '79. Anti-gunners oppose a free people's rights! Jerry Ahern.

Guns and Ammo. 23:30. N. '79. Gun control: conspiracy or deceit? Jerry Ahern.

Guns and Ammo. 23:28. D. '79. Crime control ignored by the anti-gunners! Jerry Ahern.
Guns and Ammo. 24:24 (editorial). F. '80. Tyrants seize arms, free men keep them. Jan Libouret.
Guns and Ammo. 24:30. Je. '80. The gun—ultimate symbol of self-reliance. Jerry Ahern.
Guns and Ammo. 24:6. Jl. '80. Washington report. Jim Oliver.
Guns and Ammo. 24:30. Jl. '80. Teddy plans a gun grab. Jerry Ahern.
°Harpers. 257:28+. S. '78. Against civil disarmament. Don B. Kates Jr.
Human Behavior. 7:27. My. '78. Gun control on trial: it can't protect those behind closed doors.
Journal of Criminal Law & Criminology. 70:73–6. Spring '79. Concealable firearms and ex-felons. Mogens Faber.
°Journal of Current Social Issues. 16:20. Summer '77. Living without handguns. Jack Corbett.
Journal of Political Science & Administration. 7:439–48. D. '79. Look at gun control enforcement. Paul Bendis and Steven Balkin.
°Law & Liberty. Vol. 4, No. 4, Winter '79. On turning citizens into criminals. David T. Hardy.
Law & Society Review. 13:393–430. Winter '76. Mandatory sentencing and the abolition of plea bargaining: the Michigan felony firearm statute. Milton Huemann and Colin Loftin.
McCalls. 107:67. N. '79. Do gun-control laws miss the mark? J. E. Diamond.
°MacLean's. 93:29. My. 5 '80. Gunfight at the not-O.K. Corral (gun law debate in New York). Lawrence O'Toole.
°MacLean's. 93:11. Jl. 21 '80. New York's tough gun law isn't. Lawrence O'Toole.
Nation's Cities. 2:1. N. 19, '79. Gun law reduced crime, according to LEAA survey. Wendy Serbin Smith.
National Review. 30:842. Jl. 7 '78. Who shall write the law? M. S. Evans.
°National Review. 31:1434 N. 9 '79. Crime and gun control; McClure-Volkmer bill on Federal Firearms Law Reform Act. M. S. Evans.
°New Leader. 61:7–9. S. 11, '78. Shooting down gun control. P. C. Stuart.
New Republic. 180:3. F. 10, '79. TRB from Washington.
New York. 10:38. D. 12, '77. Nice people who carry guns. Susan Hall.
New York Times. 18:1. Mr. 3, '80. Editorial.

New York Times. II, 1:4. Mr. 31, '80. Illegal guns by the millions
    filling city.
°New York Times. II, 6:3. Mr. 31, '80. The history of a handgun,
    from factory to felony.
New York Times. p A34. D. 11, '80. Reagan and handgun control
    (editorial).
Newsweek. 91:23. My. 8, '78. Why Nick? Jeanne Shields.
Outdoor Life. 161:8+. Ap. '78. Carter's gun bill: controls and has-
    sles. Richard Starnes.
Outdoor Life. 161:12+. Je. '78. Facts that help you fight for hunt-
    ing. Richard Starnes.
Outdoor Life. 163:10+. Ap. '79. Worst attack yet on hunting.
    Richard Starnes.
Outdoor Life. 163:10+. My. '79. New look at gun control. Richard
    Starnes.
Outdoor Life. 165:8+. My. '80. The crunch is on. Richard Starnes.
Outdoor Life. 164:47. Je. '80. Handgun hunting: sport or stunt?
    Jim Carmichel.
Progressive. 42:12. F. '79. Handgun menace. Wallace Terry.
°Public Interest. No 45, Fall '76, p 37–62. The great American gun
    war. B. Bruce-Briggs.
Public Opinion Quarterly. 41:427. Winter '77. Attitude measure-
    ment and the gun-control paradox. Howard Schuman.
Society. 15:4. S. '78. Gun registration; study by Howard Schuman
    and Stanley Presser.
°Sports Afield. 181:14+. Ja. '79. Guns and hunting: fact and fan-
    tasy. Grits Gresham.
St. Louis University Law Journal. Vol. 23, No. 1. '79. p 11–34.
    Some remarks on the prohibition of handguns. Don B. Kates
    Jr.
°Texas Monthly. 7:101+. Mr. '79. Have guns, will travel. Jan Reid.
US Catholic. 44:2 (editorial). Ag. '79. Sex education belongs in the
    gun store. R. E. Burns.
°USA Today. 108:8–10. Ja. '80. Handgun control and the politics
    of fear. C. J. Orasin.
°Washingtonian. 15:86. D. '79. The fat man and the gun collector.
    Joseph Goulden.